D1133211

AMERICA'S FIRST CIVILIZATION

THE SMITHSONIAN LIBRARY

AMERICA'S FIRST CIVILIZATION

by MICHAEL D. COE

Consultant

RICHARD B. WOODBURY

Curator, North American Anthropology
Smithsonian Museum of Natural History

Published by AMERICAN HERITAGE PUBLISHING CO., INC.
in association with THE SMITHSONIAN INSTITUTION

Book trade and institutional distribution by
D. VAN NOSTRAND COMPANY INC.

FRONT COVER: *A gigantic stone head, unearthed from the La Venta site, bears the "helmet" and scowling features that stamp it as Olmec. Such Colossal Heads were the first artifacts to be definitely traced to this civilization.*
FRONTISPIECE: *Found at Las Limas, Veracruz, this seated figure cradles a "baby" that is half-human, half-jaguar, a recurring Olmec motif.*
ABOVE: *Celts or small axheads were part of the jade offerings found at a La Venta tomb site. Some of the celts in this group are not only polished but incised with faces that obviously had religious meaning.*

Library of Congress Catalog Card Number: 68–55791. Printed in U.S.A.

CONTENTS

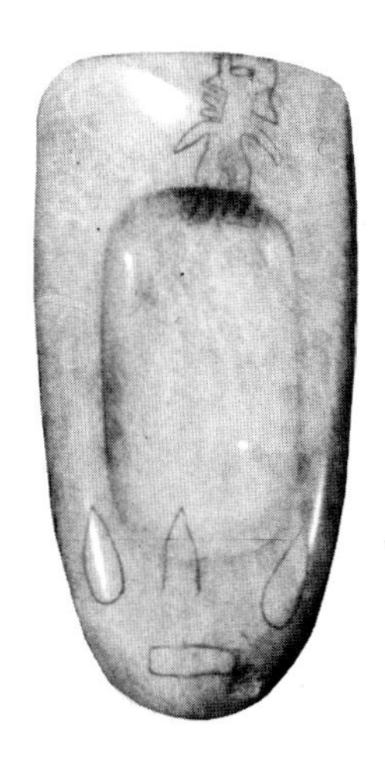

PREFACE

A pottery figure from Olmec times is probably of a male ballplayer, seen wearing protective belt and knee guards for the sacred game.

This book is about the oldest—and the strangest—of the native New World civilizations. The Olmec civilization of the southern Mexican jungles was virtually unknown to archaeologists as recently as fifty years ago, and its true importance has only just been realized. Recent and exciting research on the ancient Olmec has thrown an entirely new light on a very old problem: how the Indian peoples of our hemisphere came to be what they were—and are.

Odd though it may be, we will be describing a people whose own name for themselves we do not know. Since these "Olmec" were the very first American Indians to achieve such a high level of social, cultural, and artistic complexity, it would not be stretching a word to call them "civilized." This level was reached three thousand years ago, so far back in time that only the most fragmentary memories of such a people survived among the latest of Mexico's Pre-Columbian civilizations—the Aztec. In our own western world, it represents all the elapsed time between the Trojan War and the Atomic Age!

Between the collapse of the Olmec realm and the Spanish conquest of Mexico, a tremendous amount of history came to pass in what we now call the Old World: Buddha, Socrates, Confucius, and Christ lived and died; Classical Greece and Imperial Rome rose and fell in turn; Chaucer wrote *The Canterbury Tales;* Henry V took Agincourt; and Islam carried Sword and Book to Spain and Constantinople.

But this is not a history, for we are dealing with a people for whom there are no reliable documents (although, as will be seen, they do seem to have had a form of writing), nor even secure traditions. No Mexican Homer sings to us of the deeds of ancient Olmec heroes. So in the absence of readable accounts, we must apply the techniques of *pre*history to the Olmec. Here it is not the historians, but the archaeologists, who, armed with methods and theories that have largely come to them from the natural sciences and from anthropology, must bring to life dead and forgotten cultures.

The strength of the archaeological approach is that over long periods of time and over great expanses of the globe the relationships between groups of men and the environments with which they have had to cope can be clearly seen. It has been said of history that he who does not learn its lessons is destined to repeat its mistakes, but this can hardly be true of prehistory, for no people can be ordained to repeat, for instance, the Neolithic age. Still, certain lessons can be drawn, even new opportunities discovered, by an understanding of how early men have dealt with the possibilities and limitations of all kinds of surroundings.

Our Olmec Indians evolved a truly incredible culture in an area that would seem to us who dwell in a more temperate region as almost impossibly hostile. In the very hot, very wet, tropical lowlands of the Mexican states of Veracruz and Tabasco, amid a tangle of rivers, swamps, high jungle, and savannas, they built their great temple centers and carved huge stone monuments. It was there that the New World's first civilization arose, and we can only ask ourselves, why and how? Here the prehistorian can also apply the science of ecology—the study of the interaction between organisms and their environments—to these questions and hope to get a satisfactory answer. If we do get one, we might find a clue as to how the tropics of our now overpopulated planet could be used to best advantage.

And yet we should never allow our prehistorians' bias toward economic analysis to make us lose sight of the fact that these Olmec were people, and that unusual personalities as well as historical accidents—coincidences such as Napoleon's indigestion on the morning of Waterloo—must have played their roles. Great Olmec there certainly were, but their names and deeds will ever be unknown.

In describing the Olmec, we are also delineating one of the great culture areas of the New World, called Mesoamerica, a term used for those portions of Mexico and Central America that were civilized in pre-Spanish times. In spite of a very interesting diversity, there is also a fundamental unity among the Mesoamerican cultures, whether Maya, Toltec, Aztec, Totonac, Zapotec, or Mixtec. There are probably strong ecological reasons for the diversity. For the unity there can be but one cause: a common heritage. This heritage can only be Olmec.

Let us then examine how Olmec civilization took shape on the Gulf Coast lowlands during the centuries around one thousand years before Christ, how it flourished, and how it died. We will then see how the Olmec pattern was transmitted to become the common legacy of all the native peoples of Mesoamerica.

U.S.
Rio Grande
TAMAULIPAS
MEXICO
VERACRUZ
El Tajín
HIDALGO
Tula
Teotihuacán
TLAXCALA
Tlatilco
Mexico City
Tlapacoya
MORELOS
Las Bocas
Chalcatzingo
PUEBLA
TEHUACAN VALLEY
MICHOACAN
Balsas R.
GUERRERO
Papagayo R.
Juxtlahuaca
PACIFIC OCEAN

GULF OF MEXICO

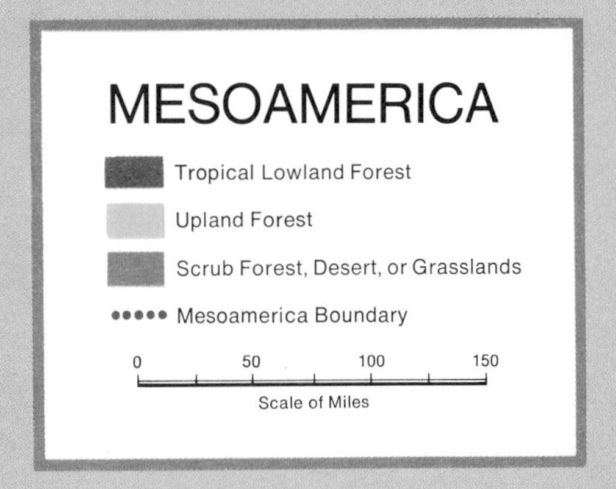

1. DISCOVERY OF THE MESOAMERICAN PAST

When Columbus sailed west to the very edge of the world, he found not the Indies but a New World, an enormous realm of land and peoples that had been effectively isolated, unknown, and even unsuspected by most of the peoples of the Old World. Almost as soon as the first contact was made, on the little island of San Salvador in the Bahamas, speculations began on who these strange, bronzed, black-haired savages might be. Columbus himself thought them "Indians," inhabitants of the East Indies, and felt confident that he was not far from Japan and might even be in the lands of the Great Khan of Cathay. By the time the Pacific Ocean had been discovered by the European explorers and the full immensity and isolation of the North and South American continents realized, the mystery of the American "Indians" was redoubled.

Following closely on these great discoveries was the Spanish conquest of Mexico and Peru. The contemptuous dismissal of the Indians as savages soon turned to an almost universal admiration as accounts, most of them accurate and detailed, of the great civilizations filtered back to European philosophers and scholars. Even the hard-bitten Spanish conquistadors were awe-struck at the size and splendor of the empires that they were smashing to ruins. Consider the letter that Cortés sent to his emperor, Charles V (dated October 30, 1520), in an attempt to describe the wonders which he had seen in the great Aztec capital of Tenochtitlán, gleaming white on an island in the midst of a broad lake. It reads in part:

A detail from an Aztec relief portrays the emperor Tizoc (left) dressed as the War God.

To give an account, Very Powerful Lord, of the greatness, and the strange and marvelous things of this great city of [Tenochtitlán] to Your Royal Excellency, and of all the dominions and splendor of Moctezuma its sovereign; of all the rites and customs which these people practice, and of the order prevailing in the government, not only of this city, but also of others belonging to this lord, much time and many very expert narrators would be required. I shall never be able to say one-hundredth part of what might be told respecting them, but, nevertheless, as far as I am able, I shall speak of some of the things I have seen, which although badly described, I know very well will cause much wonder, that they will hardly be believed, because even we, who see them here with our own eyes, are unable to comprehend their reality.

It is fortunate for us that the Cross accompanied the Sword into Mexico, for the early Spanish friars were as gifted a group of scholars as could have been found anywhere in the world at that time. And this is particularly true of the Franciscan missionaries who founded the College of the Holy Cross, in what is now Mexico City.

From the pen of one such friar, Bernardino de Sahagún, has come a great sixteenth-century encyclopedia on virtually all aspects of Aztec life as it was just before the conquest. It is by combining these works of scholarship (some of them written down by the Aztec nobles themselves) with the eyewitness reporting of the conquistadors that we are able to reconstruct with some certainty the society, politics, religion, and daily life of the Aztec civilization.

The mighty imperial city, Tenochtitlán, was so thoroughly destroyed by the Spaniards that hardly anything of it remains beneath Mexico City, the modern capital built upon its ruins. On the eve of the conquest, Tenochtitlán contained perhaps sixty thousand people. In the center of the city was the Sacred Precinct, within which were lofty temples raised upon pyramids, dedicated to the worship of the innumerable gods of the Aztec people. The never-ceasing rituals, which included the heart sacrifice of vast numbers of war captives, were in the hands of a celibate clergy. Around the Sacred Precinct were the palace of the emperor, Moctezuma II, and those of his predecessors. Beyond this were the great houses of court nobles and administrators, and farther out yet, the dwellings of the freemen and merchants.

This was the administrative heart of an empire that reached from the Gulf of Mexico to the Pacific and that held within its grasp millions of people of many diverse tongues and cultures. Trade was one of the two principal foundations of the empire, and the daily markets of the Aztec capital were on a vaster scale than anything known to the Spaniards in the Old World; in them foodstuffs, luxury products from distant areas, and even slaves were bought and sold. The other pillar of the state was conquest, and the Aztec armies were feared all over Mesoamerica for their skill at arms and for their ferocity. Conquered states were quickly incorporated into the Aztec empire and forced to pay heavy tribute in food, weapons, and other goods for the support of Tenochtitlán.

A copy of an Aztec drawing shows the conquistador Cortés arriving in Mexico in 1519, bearing the Flag, the Cross, and the Sword. For the Aztec the bearded Cortés appeared at first to be the human embodiment of the great Aztec god Quetzalcóatl, the Feathered Serpent. With his army of about 600, Cortés very shortly made clear the meaning of the Sword. But as Mesoamerican civilization crumbled before them, many Spanish missionaries and scholars began to ponder its origins.

But from where did the Aztec come? They themselves say over and over in their own histories that they were the last to enter central Mexico, to take over that vast, lake-filled valley in which they built their mighty capital. According to them, they left an ancient homeland, Aztlán, located somewhere in western or northwestern Mexico, and wandered east following the image of the tribal god carried by four priests. The year was around A.D. 1168. They were by their own testimony semibarbarians, but by the mid-fourteenth century they had settled in the Valley of Mexico and began adopting the customs of their more civilized predecessors, whose descendants still controlled small city-states around the lake.

The Aztec, in fact, readily admitted that there had been a glorious empire before their own, ruled from another capital, Tula, by a people called the Toltec. This city, which according to traditional accounts was founded in the tenth century A.D. and destroyed in the twelfth, is described in such enthusiastic terms by the Aztec that one begins to think of some "Big Rock Candy Mountain." The Toltec were said to have been the finest craftsmen who ever lived—that there was nothing they could not do. They were ruled by a great king who took on the title of the mighty Mesoamerican god Quetzalcóatl (Feathered Serpent), and the doings of this man have been forever mixed up with those more properly ascribed to the god. This semilegendary Quetzalcóatl was ousted from power by the evil god Tezcatlipoca, Ruler of Life and Death, and forced to leave Tula, journey to the Gulf Coast, and cross to the land on the other side from where he was one day to return for the redemption of the Mexican people. That a Toltec ruler calling himself Feathered Serpent did actually make this trip and did in fact conquer the land on the other side of the Gulf—Yucatán—we know from the traditions of the Maya, who inhabited Yucatán.

So, as far back as the mid-tenth century we have some kind of history, semilegendary though it is. (It is reminiscent of the *Song of Roland* and other chivalric romances having to do with the struggle of Charlemagne and the Saracens, historical in basis but thoroughly entwined with the poetry of legend.) But the Spanish scholars of the colonial period, and their readers in Europe, wanted to know what lay behind this. What *was* the ultimate origin of the American Indians? As we shall later see, the Aztec had an almost legendary remembrance of an even earlier civilization, whose great ruins lay not too many miles away from their capital; this was Teotihuacán; and beyond it, the wonderful land of Tamoanchán, where Mesoamerican civilization first began.

History, legend, or whatever one wants to call it were thus of little help in unraveling the origin of the natives and of their civilizations. Nor did the accounts of the Inca in Peru or of any other native people help much. Here in the New World, in the far-removed wilds of Mexico, was a people who had gods, temples, priests, incense, confession, and sacrifice; kings and palaces; books and writing. What more natural conclusion was there, in want of other evidence, than to bring them lock, stock, and barrel out of the civilized regions of the Old World? And,

As Spanish scholars, chiefly monks, soon surmised, Indian culture had very deep roots. From the Aztec they learned of an earlier people known as the Toltec, the immediate predecessors of the Aztec, and of the creators of a highly militaristic empire centered at Tula, to the north of modern Mexico City. This gigantic stone column from Tula represents a Toltec warrior and is one of four that once supported the roof of a temple to the Feathered Serpent.

to ease matters, the story of the ten lost tribes of Israel was tailor-made for such an explanation—the Indians were Jews.

Every conceivable voyage and migration account from the Old World, no matter how fantastic, was searched in the sixteenth to nineteenth centuries for clues of this nature. The natives of the New World had come from Wales with the legendary King Madoc; they were Tartars from China (this one was not so far from the mark); and so on. Only a few scholars cautioned against such wild speculations, among them, José de Acosta, a Spanish missionary who proposed in 1590 that the American Indians were Asiatics by origin who had crossed into North America by land from northeast Asia. But who would have dared to suggest, at a time when the earth itself was not thought to be more than five or six thousand years old, that this initial peopling might have happened ten, twenty, or forty thousand years ago?

It was not very long after the conquest of 1521 that travelers in colonial Mexico and Central America stumbled across remains of other, older civilizations. Teotihuacán, near Mexico City, had never in fact been forgotten, and its ruins are so imposing that it is unlikely they would ever have been. Moctezuma made an annual pilgrimage on foot to its immense Pyramid of the Sun. Beside Teotihuacán, the principal Mesoamerican civilization discovered in post-conquest times was that of the Maya.

The Maya is popularly thought of as one of the "dead" civilizations of the world, but it was very much alive at the time of Spanish contact and has really never completely died, surviving today in varying degrees of purity among the approximately two million living Mayan-speakers. In the mid-sixteenth century, as now, they inhabited two areas: the northern part of the Yucatán Peninsula and the rough mountain country of Guatemala and Chiapas (in southeastern Mexico). All of the lowland jungle in between was an empty wilderness.

One of the most interesting and terrifying figures of colonial Mexico was the Franciscan Bishop of Yucatán, Fray Diego de Landa. Famed for allegedly destroying all the extant Maya books or codices in a great bonfire in the 1550's, he was nonetheless the man who set down on paper much of what we know of Maya civilization as it was just before the Spanish arrival. This great work was, however, lost to scholarship until the manuscript was rediscovered in the 1860's. Like numerous other friars, Landa noted that the flatland of Yucatán was dotted with ruins left by a past civilization, and he did much to connect them with the ancestors of the living Maya. He was also fascinated by the Maya system of hieroglyphic writing and by the complex Maya calendar, and he left many clues for their subsequent decipherment.

Thus, the Maya were never truly unknown. But it was not until the nineteenth century that the travels of two men first brought to the world the full glories of the ancient Maya civilization. John Lloyd Stephens was an American lawyer, diplomat, and inveterate traveler, and his companion of two momentous journeys was Frederick Catherwood, an Eng-

lish artist and draftsman. The first of their trips, in 1839, took them, mainly on foot or by the most primitive means of transport, into the fringes of the vast, deserted central area that proved to be full of abandoned Maya centers, as well as to many of the ruins of Yucatán.

Then in 1841 they returned to Yucatán for a more thorough reconnaissance. The descriptions of Stephens and the illustrations by Catherwood, which they published jointly in *Incidents of Travel in Central America, Chiapas, and Yucatán*, can hardly be surpassed for accuracy and for cool scholarship. They knew that the great archaeological sites which we now ascribe to the Classic period were the works of Maya Indians, and not of Israelites, Welshmen, or Tartars, and they did all they could to determine their age.

Unfortunately, in their day the study of the Maya hieroglyphs and calendar had scarcely begun. The true antiquity of the ancient centers of the Maya lowlands was only determined after the calendrical part of the Classic Maya inscriptions had been fully deciphered. The inscribed stone monuments of the lowland Maya sites have a system of dating called the Long Count, an exact, daily count reckoned from some mythical point in the distant past. Once this was understood, by the close of the nineteenth century, the problem naturally became one of correlating the Maya calendar with our own. Many specialists have worked on this problem with differing results, but the most generally accepted correlation would place the period within which most of the Maya centers reached their full form as begin-

Greatest by far of ancient Mesoamerican cities was Teotihuacán, northeast of Mexico City. At its peak, Teotihuacán covered an area of about eight square miles and was home for at least 100,000 people. Built from about the time of Christ to A.D. *600, it was the most powerful political and cultural force in all Mesoamerica during what is known as the Classic stage. To the Aztec, who knew only that Teotihuacán had preceded the Toltec, it could only have been*

built by gods or giants. They knew nothing of its creators, the language they spoke, or the name they went by, and to date modern scientists know no more. The site is dominated by two tremendous pyramids, one traditionally dedicated to the Sun God, the other to the Goddess of the Moon (below), and by a temple to the Feathered Serpent, a representation of which is shown at left. The city was violently destroyed sometime after A.D. *650 at the hands of an unknown enemy.*

The first serious scholars to explore the ruins of ancient Mesoamerica were John Lloyd Stephens, an American lawyer, and Frederick Catherwood, an English artist. Arriving in Central America in 1839, they systematically reconnoitered the almost totally unknown remains of that most advanced of New World civilizations, the Maya. This lithograph by Catherwood depicts two of their party hunting a jaguar beneath a Maya pyramid at Izamal, in Yucatán.

ning slightly before A.D. 300 and ending around A.D. 900. The solving of the problem of the Maya Long Count has thus given to archaeologists the only absolute, day-by-day chronology that exists for Mesoamerica.

As ancient Mexican and Central American cultures were encountered and described, such as the Zapotec civilization of Oaxaca, or the Totonac ruins of El Tajín in the forested lowlands of north-central Veracruz, every effort was made to cross-date them with the Maya, so that the Maya time scale could be applied to their own chronology.

By the early decades of our century, it had become quite clear that the golden age of Mesoamerica was reached, not in the centuries just preceding the conquest, but long before that, in what we call the Classic. But what lay in back of the Classic? Such civilizations could not just have appeared out of thin air. And, with a few eccentric exceptions, no scholars by this time could believe in the old migration theories, mainly because the New World cultures were found to have been so different from those of the Old in form and in content; most importantly, the Mesoamerican food complex was built on plants like maize, the common bean, and the squash, none of which were known in the Old World before Columbus. All of these facts argued that the natives of the New World had been there for a very long time, and that the civilizations of Mesoamerica must have been presaged by a lengthy period of development.

The true time span involved and the working out of the details of this gestation period had to wait for the birth of modern archaeology, based upon the principle of stratigraphy. Simply stated, this means that archaeological deposits usually occur in well-marked layers or strata, and that the deeper the layer in which an object is embedded, the older it is. It was taken over by British archaeologists in the late nineteenth century from the geologists and, as in geology, the application of stratigraphic methods is often considerably more complex than one might suspect from the principle. The ideal stratigraphic situation is an undisturbed refuse heap in use over many generations; here, careful excavations successively peeling layer from layer would show gradual changes in discarded cultural items from top to bottom, or from later to earlier.

For instance, a modern American city garbage dump might begin on bedrock with broken kerosene lamps and end up in the topmost stratum with fragments of fluorescent tubing. However, all kinds of disturbances of the stratigraphic record can happen at any time, such as the cutting down of storage pits, or the placing of burials, or the digging of trenches for building foundations. Only after considerable experience in archaeological digging can one interpret such confusing situations.

It took a long time for such an obvious principle to be applied to New World archaeology. It was not until 1914 that an American archaeologist, Nels Nelson, tried it out on the refuse heaps or middens of the Pueblo Indians in our own Southwest, giving a prehistoric past where there had been none at all. Nelson, like his predecessors in England, realized the value

OVERLEAF: *One of the many colored lithographs published by Catherwood shows a small pyramid in the center of a Late Maya town, Tulum, which was built on the edge of a cliff overlooking the Caribbean on the eastern coast of the Yucatán Peninsula. It is quite possible that Tulum was still a viable community at the time the conquistadors arrived, for they later wrote of sighting from the sea a white-walled citadel, which they called Great Cairo.*

of pottery fragments or potsherds for establishing a sequence of cultural changes, for nothing changes so fast, is so breakable, or so nearly universal as pottery.

Nelson, however, was "scooped" in the use of stratigraphy by the Mexican anthropologist Manuel Gamio, who four years before made a deep cut in refuse layers in a site close to Mexico City. This simple excavation turned up no hidden treasure, no rich tombs, no buried temples, but something more important: the first *stratified* record of the peoples who had occupied the Valley of Mexico over a period of fifteen hundred years. At the top, obviously, were sherds and other artifacts of the Aztec civilization. Below this was refuse containing fragments of pottery of types known to come from the ruins of Teotihuacán.

And, finally, at very deep levels, much simpler kinds of pottery and small handmade clay figurines of a culture that Gamio and others then called "Archaic" and which was thus proved to be even older than Teotihuacán. At one stroke he had established a *relative* chronology (incomplete, as we now know) for the Valley of Mexico: Archaic, followed by the Teotihuacán civilization, followed by the Aztec. In the next few decades it was discovered that Toltec remains belonged between Teotihuacán and Aztec. In a way, then, the old chronicles of the Aztec had been correct.

Eventually, stratigraphic excavations were made over much of Mesoamerica, including the abandoned centers of the Classic Maya, and a remarkable picture emerged of the long, prehistoric sequence that went to make Mesoamerica. But all of this, with the exception of those ruins directly dated by the Maya Long Count calendar, was *relative;* that is, all that one could say was that culture A was older than culture B, which was in turn prior to culture C. But how much older?

The native "historical" chronicles were unfortunately hard to interpret, since they were based upon a kind of permutating chronology —a recurring cycle of fifty-two years—not tied to a consecutive time count, so that Teotihuacán, for instance, was hard to place in terms of our Christian calendar. In 1945 there were few archaeologists who would have placed it earlier than A.D. 600, as we now know it to be; and there were even fewer who would have put the beginning of the pre-Teotihuacán, Archaic cultures much earlier than the time of Christ.

What was clearly needed was some kind of *absolute* dating, independent of native calendars, which would furnish dates in terms of our own calendar. The discovery of the radiocarbon method was developed in the late 1940's by the American chemist, Willard Libby, for which he received the 1960 Nobel Prize. In the years since, radioactive dating has revolutionized the technique of archaeology and our understanding of prehistory, all over the inhabited world.

This remarkable "clock" is based upon the circumstance that a radioactive isotope of carbon, C^{14}, is present in all living things. After the death of an organism, whether man, fish, or tree, this radioactive carbon decomposes at a known rate. After 5,568 years, one half is gone; after another 5,568 years, one half of this; and so on by halves until there is too little

The chart illustrates the slow pace of cultural evolution in Mesoamerica. As in the Old World, it was many thousands of years after the introduction of primitive agriculture that village life began. However, once settled communities appeared, the pace picked up, and it was not long before the start of the first civilization, in this case, the Olmec. The transitional points on the right side of the chart up to the Classic stage are based on radiocarbon dating.

to measure in the elaborate Geiger counters used for this purpose. By measuring the activity of the C^{14} in a sample of charcoal from an ancient hearth, for instance, one can determine within a certain degree of statistical reliability the number of years ago the tree from which the firewood came was cut. Not only charcoal, but wood, bone, shell, cloth, and many other organic substances as much as sixty or seventy thousand years old can be so dated by the C^{14} method. We shall see what the results were when it was applied to New World, and more especially to Mesoamerican, archaeology and to the Olmec.

The radiocarbon clock has at last let us see the full time depth of the American past. From this vantage point, it is clear that Mesoamerica, as with other great cultural hearths like the Near East, has advanced through a series of stages, or developmental levels, although not everybody exactly agrees as to what they were. A *stage* is by no means the same thing as a *period*, which refers only to a span of time. To take an analogy, all of us on this planet are now in the twentieth century, which is a period. A few nations are now in the Atomic Age, which is a stage; others have barely passed the Industrial Revolution, which is another stage; and many thousand natives of the New Guinea interior can be said to be in the Neolithic stage, which our ancestors left behind over four thousand years ago. On a world scale, "progress" is thus a mosaic, with steps forward coming in scattered bits and pieces.

And so it was in Mesoamerica. A scheme of stages based upon many years of stratigraphic excavation and upon C^{14} dating is now generally agreed upon, but we must realize that not all regions within this vast area went through them at the same time. For instance, western Mexico probably never did achieve the Classic stage. For the present, though, five stages are generally accepted.

The original ancestors of the American Indians are now known to have crossed the barren, snow-swept land bridge that existed between Siberia and Alaska during the Ice Age, or Pleistocene epoch. Whether the first bands of wandering hunters came over twelve, twenty, or forty thousand years ago is not known. But some time before 9000 B.C. these primitive hunters had reached the North American continent; stone-tipped spears and darts were used to hunt the great herbivores—especially mammoths and mastodons—until the retreat of the northern glaciers after 8000 B.C.

Archaic is now used to describe the early stage of food-collecting eked out with primitive agriculture, to be described in the following chapter. This stage lasted in Mesoamerica from 7000 to about 1500 B.C.

What we now call the Formative stage was in the days of Gamio and other pioneer Mexican archaeologists called the Archaic. We use Formative for a pre-Classic stage of intensified village life, with pottery, textiles, and all of the other "Neolithic" arts, lasting until A.D. 200 or 300. Of which more anon.

The Classic, or so-called Golden Age of Mesoamerica, was the stage of great civilizations and great art, lasting from the end of the Formative until A.D. 900. By no accident, this also hap-

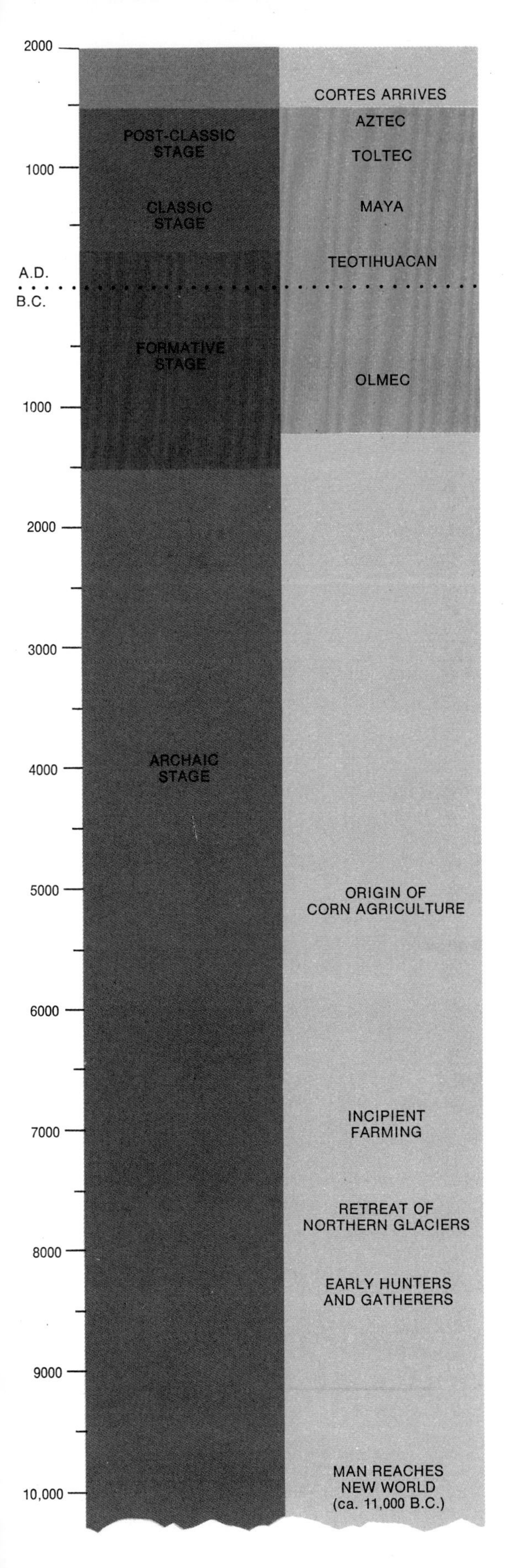

pened to be the span, or period, during which the Maya were carving their stone monuments with Long Count dates, and we may thus be confusing period with stage. We now know, for instance, that Teotihuacán civilization, always included in the Classic, began *before* A.D. 200 and was pretty much finished by A.D. 600.

There is little doubt that by A.D. 900 most, or all, of the Classic civilizations were falling or had already fallen into ruins: Maya, Teotihuacán, Monte Albán, and so on. The Classic was succeeded by the Post-Classic, a new urban stage in which militarism became a way of life, and great conquest states, first the Toltec, then the Aztec, arose. The Post-Classic came to an end with the arrival of Cortés. Or is this stage, too, a fiction? For this also happened to be the time period for which we have detailed accounts from the Spanish friars and native nobility. Many archaeologists suspect that the Classic civilizations were just as bloodthirsty and conquest-bent as those of the Post-Classic.

This, then, is the orderly scheme that has met with general acceptance, probably because it fits comfortably with a view of human cultural development as gradual and ordered: that is, progress is seen as a line of development gently sloping ever upward. For that reason, probably few archaeologists have been prepared for the disturbance which the discovery of the Olmec has played with that neat curve: a Classic civilization right at the very start of the Formative! To understand what this means, we must turn back to the food-producing "revolution" in Mesoamerica, which made the Olmec possible in the first place.

2. NOMADS BECOME SETTLED FARMERS

Nomads never achieve civilization by themselves. A fully sedentary way of life is the only passport to a complex culture, including that of the Olmec. For a people to stay in the same place the year round, whether in village, town, or city, a constant supply of food must either be immediately at hand, storable over the lean months, or easily transportable from elsewhere. Otherwise, for at least part of the year, the inhabitants are going to have to move to some other place.

The most efficient way to achieve this state of "sedentism" is by the domestication of plants, that is, by harnessing the food energy stored in plants, usually contained within their seeds, to man's own ends. This has been brought about in both Old and New Worlds by a process of selection that has ended in the "capture" of the plants themselves, that is, they have become incapable of propagating themselves and require the presence of man to reproduce. The seedless banana is a well-known example of this, but it is also true of the important cereal grasses—wheat, barley, oats, and rice—that were the basis of the "Neolithic Revolution," which began about 7800 B.C. in the Near and Far East. But whoever reaps must also sow. The process ending in this capture was, however, completely unwitting. Let us take a hypothetical example of how this might have come about.

A primitive band of collectors comes every year to a valley where a certain wild grass with edible seeds grows. They collect these seeds by cutting off the heads of mature plants with crude sickles; but it is typical of wild grasses

Corn, the staple crop of Mesoamerica, grows beside a back road in Guerrero, Mexico.

(like the wild ancestor of wheat) that the seeds are attached by bracts that become brittle when ripe, so that in nature the plants shed their seeds in a high wind. Thus the blow of a sickle or the breaking off of the head by hand makes most of the normally attached grains fall to the ground, while the "defective" ones, growing on mutant plants with tougher bracts, have a greater chance of being taken back to camp by the collector.

Eventually, in the refuse around the camp of this band, there springs up a wild grass population of defective plants that have tough rather than brittle attachments for the seeds. The critical point in domestication is reached when someone gets the idea to try planting the seeds from these in a garden patch or field that he keeps weeded. The end result is a captive food plant that can truly be considered domesticated.

There would obviously be all sorts of variations on this oversimplified scheme. Root crops, for instance, are propagated by cuttings or shoots, and the selection is for larger, starch-rich tubers. And some domesticates in the world, like certain fruit trees, are less captive than others, in the sense that under certain conditions they can exist in the wild state. But, as the Russian geneticist N. I. Vavilov has pointed out, the evolution of all domesticates (and this includes animals) is to some extent directed by man.

Settled life in Mesoamerica was dependent upon an impressive array of plants, while the number of animals harnessed to the service of man was correspondingly small. Only the dog, turkey, Muscovy duck, and stingless honeybee were so tamed, a striking contrast to the role that animal husbandry played among the Old World cultures. Consider, however, the domestic plants that Mesoamerica or its neighbors gave to the rest of mankind after 1492: Indian corn or maize, the bean (black or navy), squash and pumpkin, tomato, sweet potato, chili pepper, avocado, cacao (chocolate), and vanilla bean. South America contributed the white or "Irish" potato, the lima bean, and manioc or cassava (used to make tapioca). It is hard to conceive of European cuisine before the arrival of these plants, some of which had been under cultivation by the American Indians for thousands of years before the Spanish conquest.

The key, however, to the understanding of Mesoamerican civilization is corn. Where it flourished, so also did high culture; where it produced but scanty yields (as in many parts of western and northern Mexico), native civilization was nonexistent. Maya, Aztec, Toltec, or Olmec—all depended upon this staff of life.

It has long been thought that by finding the time and place of its domestication, one would discover the origin of civilization itself in this part of the world. But the origin of corn has long been a mystery since, unlike most of the important food cereals known to man, it has no living wild progenitor. As it is now in all its variety, corn is a total captive, unable, because of the long husks that completely enclose the ripe ear, to disperse its seeds unaided by man. Corn is a grass, a giant grass; its male flower or tassel bears the pollen, while the female organ of the plant, the ear, bears the seeds. Under human

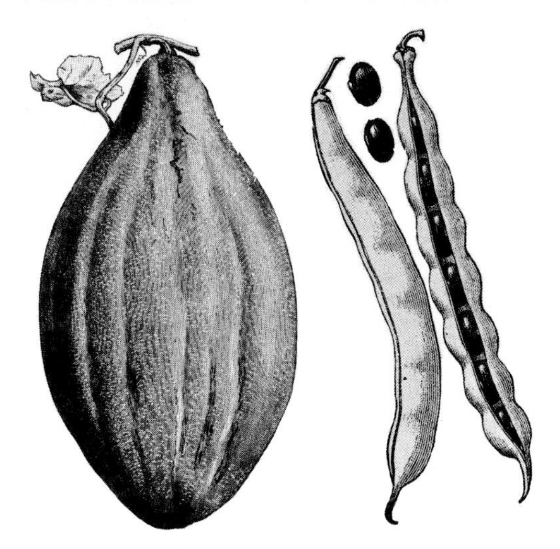

Archaeological studies of Mesoamerica, involving scientists from many disciplines, have shown the area to be one of the world's principal "hearths" of plant domestication. By controlling the evolution of plants over thousands of years, man in Mesoamerica produced such now familiar foods as the pumpkin, squash, and bean, none of which were known to the Old World. These were the primary sources of energy that made possible all settled life in the region.

selection the ear has become enormous, a great repository of food energy. The end result is that corn is now known to be the most productive food plant on earth.

How did this strange situation come about, when and where? The mystery's solution (which was arrived at in the 1950's and 1960's) is the result of a long collaboration between a botanist, Dr. Paul C. Mangelsdorf, the leading authority on corn, and Dr. Richard "Scotty" MacNeish, an archaeologist. It has long been known that corn has two close relatives among the grasses that grow in Mesoamerica. One is *Tripsacum,* a grass widespread in the Western Hemisphere. The other is teosinte, which grows as an unwanted weed in Indian cornfields of Guatemala and western Mexico and which looks remarkably like corn itself. Earlier archaeologists and botanists thought that teosinte was the wild ancestor they had been seeking, and that since it is common among the Maya Indians of Guatemala, the Maya had then been the first to domesticate corn and achieve settled life and its sequel, civilization.

By his studies of maize cytology and genetics, and by careful experiments in breeding, Mangelsdorf was able to demolish this theory. Instead, he showed that teosinte was the hybrid offspring of domestic corn and *Tripsacum,* and that the ancient ancestor of corn was corn—a wild corn that was capable of dispersing its seeds.

What kind of a corn would this have been? Here Mangelsdorf demonstrated that it would have had the characteristics of modern *pop* corn, which has small, hard seeds, and other traits to be found in *pod* corn. All Americans know pop corn, but few have seen pod corn. This strange variety is grown by some South American Indians and is often considered sacred by them. It has a gene that produces long chaff or glumes, enclosing each seed, and considerably reduced husks. By crossing the two kinds of corn, Mangelsdorf produced what he considered a good candidate for what wild maize should have looked like: a small plant with only one or two tiny ears with hard grains, the glumes long, and the husks opening up on maturation to let the seeds be dispersed by birds or by falling off. That much established, it only remained to find where and when the American Indian took this unprepossessing grass and converted it to the world's most important food plant. For this we must turn to the work of Scotty MacNeish.

From a valley only eighty miles long and twenty miles wide, completely bereft of the spectacular ruins that attract tourists to Mexico, has come some of the most exciting archaeological news in the world. This is the Tehuacán Valley of southern Puebla and northern Oaxaca, in the highlands of Mexico. Except where sugar cane is raised by modern irrigation methods, it is about as dry as a Mexican valley can be, its bottom lands covered with cactus, scrub, or thorn forest. And just why should it be a semidesert, when only a few miles to the east begin the lush, green forests of Veracruz? Because as the warm trade winds, which blow in from the northeast month after month, rise up the highland escarpment that fronts the Gulf Coast plains, they release their moisture

Richard "Scotty" MacNeish, a renowned American archaeologist who has established a whole new cultural stage for Mesoamerica (the Archaic), is seen standing in an excavation within Coxcatlán Cave, in the Tehuacán Valley. Clearly shown by the archaeologist's "cut" are "living floors" (levels of occupation) piled one on top of the other, with each full of vegetable remains and ancient cooking hearths (Dr. MacNeish is pointing to one that is particularly well defined).

upon these east-facing slopes, leaving Tehuacán Valley to the west in a rain shadow.

Just as Heinrich Schliemann was drawn to the site of ancient Troy because he believed Homer's saga told of real places, so MacNeish was drawn to Tehuacán, where there were bone-dry caves in a desiccated environment. It was in such caves and rock shelters that he felt certain of finding preserved food remains as evidence for the "food-producing revolution" in Mesoamerica. Scotty MacNeish, a Chicago-trained archaeologist, had spent many years in this quest, digging in dusty caves and rock shelters in some of the most inhospitable surroundings imaginable. For this, he has been rewarded with the discovery of a whole new developmental stage in New World prehistory, an achievement that few other archaeologists can match.

MacNeish was led to Tehuacán in a somewhat roundabout way. In 1945–1946, as a graduate student getting material for his doctoral dissertation, he was in the dry and hot state of Tamaulipas in northeastern Mexico. Although actually looking for connections between the native cultures of Mexico and the southeastern United States, he found that there were shallow caves in the Tamaulipas hills and mountains with organic remains preserved by the very dryness of the deposits. His interests quickly changed, and the possibility struck him of finding what had up to that time only been postulated but never demonstrated: a preceramic, pre-Formative stage, within which the Mesoamerican Indians would have gradually brought into domestication all or most of their important food plants—maize, beans, and squashes.

In 1948 he returned to Tamaulipas and struck archaeological "pay dirt"—a long, preceramic sequence, estimated to have lasted from 7000 to 1500 B.C. on the basis of radiocarbon dating and cultural comparison. The Indians of this time were definitely seminomadic collectors and hunters of small game, but they were proved to have had domestic plants. The oldest of these was the bottle gourd, already planted by them somewhere around 6500 B.C. and therefore probably the oldest of the New World domesticates. By about 3500 B.C., the pumpkin, two kinds of beans, and chili peppers were being grown and eaten.

Overshadowing all of these was the find of tiny corncobs in La Perra Cave, within a canyon of the Sierra de Tamaulipas. These cobs, associated with a preceramic culture dated to about 2500 B.C., are from a pop corn with tiny ears. Whether it was wild or cultivated was hard to ascertain, and only a botanist could find the answer. Very similar cobs on about the same time level had also turned up in caves of northern Mexico and in the southwestern United States. All evidence pointed to an origin in central Mexico or even farther south. Added to this was one very important piece of data. Pollen taken from a deep core drilled under what is now Mexico City showed that wild corn had flourished in the Valley of Mexico eighty thousand years ago, far back in the Ice Age and many millennia before the arrival of man in the New World.

In 1959, MacNeish conducted excavations

At right is a schematic cross section of the Tehuacán Valley. It shows the very latest approach by archaeologists to the study of a major area of occupation. Here the area is broken down into small environmental zones, or microenvironments. By determining the ecology, both ancient and contemporary, of each zone, the archaeologists can better interpret the remains uncovered in terms of how ancient man survived in the whole valley, and how much he had to move about to do so.

and pollen studies in the dry Santa Marta Cave of southeastern Chiapas, Mexico, on the border of Maya country. Here, maize turned up in the record still more recently than in Tamaulipas. Clearly, the place to look for corn's homeland was somewhere in between. After a long search for likely places, he hit upon the Tehuacán Valley. On January 21, 1960, he made a small test cut in one of the caves under the cliffs flanking the valley, bringing to light some tiny corncobs. The layer in which they were found produced charcoal that was later dated to about 3600 B.C. This, then, was the oldest corn known. A successful archaeologist, like a good general, must know when to commit all his forces. MacNeish made the decision to begin a three-year program of excavations right in the Tehuacán Valley.

From its start, the Tehuacán Project was interdisciplinary: modern archaeology demands assistance from the sister sciences, such as geology, botany, and zoology, in identifying archaeological remains, interpreting ancient ecological situations, and in reconstructing past environments, trade routes, and the like. Mangelsdorf, of course, was very much part of the project. In addition, MacNeish's team included C. Earle Smith, a botanist responsible for identification of plant foods in the refuse and for making a survey of the present-day flora of the valley so that certain foodstuffs could be correlated to place and season. Zoology was represented by Kent V. Flannery (now with the University of Michigan). Since the accurate identification of animal bones requires a good comparative skeletal collection, Flannery had to collect modern animals from different places in the valley and in the surrounding hills; in the process of so doing, he arrived at an understanding of how the past inhabitants might have caught these animals, and where and in what season.

Perhaps the most unusual expert on the project was Eric O. Callen of McGill University, a specialist in the analysis of human feces. The end products of ancient diets were very common in the caves, for these Indians had not been sanitation-minded. By reconstituting these specimens and examining them under magnification, Callen was able to identify tissues of plants and animals eaten centuries ago by the Tehuacán people. Comparing Callen's findings with the amount of bone and vegetable refuse in his excavations, MacNeish was able to estimate with some degree of accuracy the relative proportions of different foodstuffs in the ancient diet. Other studies included analysis of stone and ceramic artifacts; identification of ancient plant pollen in the cave layers; and, of course, radiocarbon analysis.

The first job of an archaeological project is to look for sites, and the first question asked of an archaeologist is how he finds them. The answer is footwork: slogging over many miles of desert or jungle, or what have you, looking for places where artifacts are common on the surface, whether they be broken potsherds, flint chips, or rusty tin cans. All of these are telltale signs that people have once lived in a particular place. MacNeish and his assistant, Frederick A. Peterson, walked up and down the hot, dusty Tehuacán Valley, picking up arti-

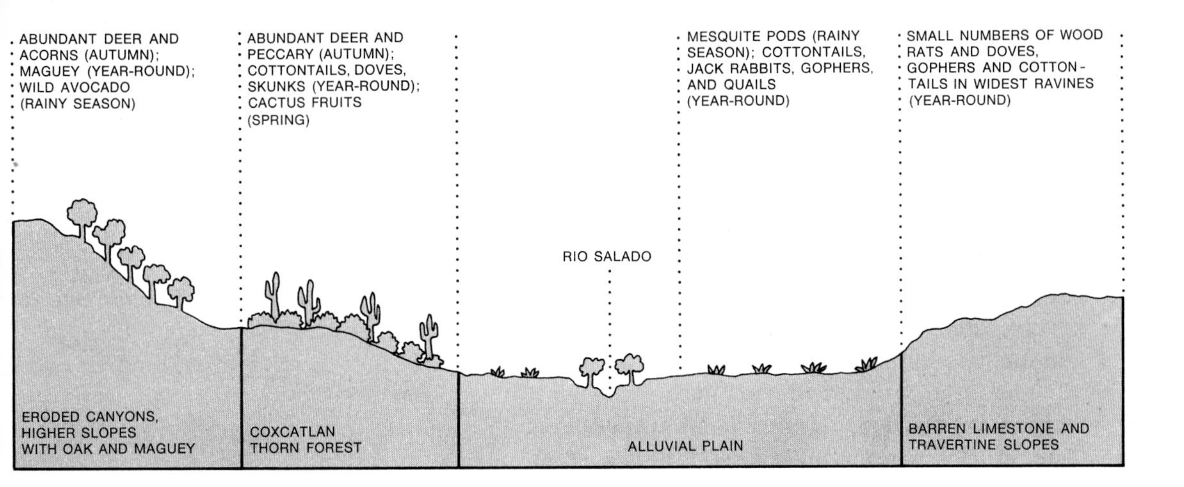

facts and climbing into caves and rock shelters. In the end, they had located 454 archaeological sites, ranging from temporary camps to what might be described as cities. Of these, they chose a small number for test excavations, to find out what the depth of occupation was and how well preserved plant remains might be. Finally, twelve sites were selected for intensive excavation, of which five were large but shallow caves.

Caves are not easy to dig. Other than the constant bother of dust raised by excavation, and the almost unbearable heat when the sun strikes these rock shelters full on, the occupation layers—old living floors, refuse layers, hearths, and so forth—are sometimes very thin and hard to follow. Furthermore, the digging of storage pits and the placing of burials—for caves were favored as cemeteries by some Mexican Indians—often make the stratigraphy even more confusing. It takes an expert with long digging experience to properly strip these layers off in their correct order. Over the years, MacNeish has worked out a technique, which he used in the Tehuacán caves, excavating in alternate squares so that he could always "read" the stratigraphic profiles on the vertical surfaces before he took off a layer.

By 1964, when excavations ended, MacNeish had found the longest and most complete archaeological sequence yet known in this continent, which included the whole story of the domestication of corn and the move toward settled life. This story opens with the Ajuereado phase, estimated to end by 6500 B.C. and probably beginning three or four thousand years before that. Instead of the cactus and scrub seen today around Tehuacán, the valley was then covered by a steppe-like, mesquite-studded grassland probably not very different from western Texas today. Certainly, the climate was somewhat cooler than it is now. Speaking of the culture of the first Indians to roam about the valley, MacNeish points out, the people were not so much "big game hunters" as collectors of wild plants and hunters of small game like gophers and rats. From time to time the small bands got together long enough to engage in communal drives for jack rabbits and antelope, but in general this was a far cry from the large-scale hunting of great animals like mammoth and bison being carried out at that time by the Indians of the western United States.

A critical point was reached in MacNeish's next phase, El Riego (6500–5000 B.C.). With the climate now returning to what we would think of as "normal" following the end of the last stage of the Ice Age, the valley took on its present appearance. Apparently, with the withdrawal of antelope and jack rabbits farther north, people came together in larger groups not so much for communal hunting as for the exploitation of vegetable foods that became abundant seasonally in some parts of the valley. One of the plants they were eating was wild squash, collected for its edible seeds rather than for the extremely bitter flesh. At some point in this remote epoch, three thousand years before the building of the Egyptian pyramids, some Tehuacán Indian thought of planting these seeds in the ground, later returning

to harvest a crop. (It will be recalled that the mere act of systematic collection can result in a partially captive population.)

So we have reached the threshold of plant domestication, of the so-called food-producing revolution in the New World. With this example before them, other species such as chili peppers, avocados, and cotton (raised for its seeds rather than for its lint) seem to have soon come under cultivation.

As the Tehuacán population grew, it began to add more and more plant foods to its diet. By the Coxcatlán phase (5000–3500 B.C.), they were exploiting a wild grass that seems, heretofore, to have been ignored: corn. Tiny cobs, hardly bigger than the filter of a cigarette, were sifted out of the refuse from Coxcatlán levels in the Tehuacán caves, and Mangelsdorf achieved his lifelong dream—wild corn had been discovered.

As Mangelsdorf had predicted, this corn was a tiny-eared grass, with long glumes like pod corn and small hard seeds like pop corn. The tassel was at the top of the ear, rather than surmounting the entire stalk, as in modern corn. And there were only two husks, which parted so that the seeds could really be dispersed in the wild state. We hear much about the glories of Maya astronomy, the marvels of the Inca highway system, and the massiveness of the Teotihuacán pyramids, but these are nothing compared to the achievement of the Coxcatlán-phase people, who made the most important discovery ever attained by the American Indians. For this plant created and fed native New World civilization.

The rest of the Tehuacán story, until we arrive at the eve of the Formative stage at 1500 B.C., is one of increasing sedentism—the expansion of agriculture allowed settlements to be occupied for much of the year—and the gradual addition of the arts of settled life. By MacNeish's Abejas phase (3500–2300 B.C.), there was enough food available from the corn, squashes, beans, and other plants grown (some of these perhaps from Tamaulipas), supplemented by the collecting of wild "crops," to allow for the establishing of little hamlets out on the valley floors. These consisted of small, circular pit houses, presumably with pole-and-thatch roofs.

Of the domestic arts, pottery has a particularly interesting history. Throughout the Archaic stage in Tehuacán, ground-stone mortars and pestles were important in the preparation of food. There is a gradual alteration of these mortars through time until by the Abejas phase they have taken on the form of stone bowls; with metal tools totally absent, their manufacture must have represented an incredible amount of work. The solution to the dilemma—the increased need for cooking vessels and containers—came in the Purrón phase (2300–1500 B.C.): someone hit upon the idea of taking clay and shaping it to imitate the stone prototypes, then baking it in a fire until it became hard. We have here the oldest pottery known so far for Mesoamerica.

Let us see how far we have come in the Tehuacán Valley. We have begun with simple bands of hunting and collecting Indians. Some six or seven thousand years later, these Indians

The search for an ancestor of modern corn led to a spectacularly successful collaboration between a botanist and an archaeologist. Paul C. Mangelsdorf, a botanist from Harvard University, had worked out a theory on corn ancestry indicating that the then accepted progenitor of teosinte (middle left) was in fact the offspring of corn and its close relative Tripsacum *(near left). Mangelsdorf held that the still undiscovered forebear would be a tiny-eared plant with husks that opened to disperse the seeds and the tassel mounted on top of the ear. A dramatic confirmation of his ideas came in 1960 when Scotty MacNeish, who had been working closely with Mangelsdorf, unearthed in a Tehuacán cave the first cob of wild corn ever seen (below). An artist's reconstruction (far left) shows it to have been almost exactly as Mangelsdorf had predicted. From such an unprepossessing plant, modern corn, the most productive food plant in the world, is descended.*

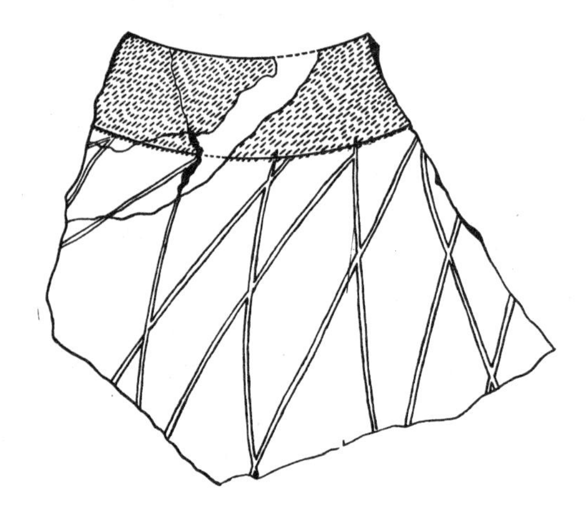

Solid evidence for the earliest fully settled village life in Mesoamerica (dating from about 1300 B.C.) was discovered by the author in 1958 at La Victoria, near the fishing village of Ocós on the Pacific Coast of Guatemala. Simple stone tools and bits of quite elaborate pottery were uncovered from an earth mound formed by the building-up of hut floors over many centuries. The fragments at right, red-painted inside, are incised with crosshatching outside; that at left is decorated with a band of paint.

have practically all of the domesticated plants ever known to Mesoamerica; they have basketry and pottery and perhaps loom-woven textiles, along with simple villages.

What, then, is lacking? For one thing, fully settled life. For another, civilization. The point is that civilization is dependent upon complete sedentism, and this in turn upon the domestication of plants and animals, but that the places and times where each was first achieved may be widely separated. This is a theme that we shall be following up elsewhere in this book. Remember that the Tehuacán Valley in 1500 B.C. had the same climate as today; today, this is a semidesert. Less than twenty-four inches of rain falls in a year, most of it in a two-month period. Without irrigation, corn production would have been pretty much confined to the river bottoms, and evidence for dams and irrigation canals does not appear at Tehuacán until after 800 B.C. Such poor production must have forced even the Purrón-phase Indians to move out of their villages for part of the year to subsist on wild-plant foods in other valley "niches."

We have here a paradox. These are the very conditions that have allowed plant remains to be preserved and so have given us an almost complete picture of the Neolithic Revolution in the New World. But they are not the conditions under which *effective* village farming—in which villages are permanently occupied—develops. For this critical point of Mesoamerican prehistory we move from the dry Mexican highlands to a totally different milieu: the hot, wet, jungle-green lowlands of the Gulf and Pacific coasts, where ancient food remains have been preserved only by lucky accident, and then only rarely.

Mesoamerica has not one but three lowlands. The greatest of these in area and, to be truthful, in its total significance (for here Maya civilization reached its height) includes the huge, flat Yucatán Peninsula and the somewhat hillier country of northern Guatemala and British Honduras lying just to the south. We are, however, now concerned with the remaining two: the broad, coastal plain fronting the Gulf Coast of Mexico, and, on the other side of the Isthmus of Tehuantepec, a narrow littoral extending down along the Pacific shore of Chiapas and Guatemala. Hot and humid, with deep alluvium deposited annually by the sluggish rivers that leap from their banks in the rainy season and snake across the land, these swampy coasts are the places where truly effective village farming was finally reached.

Part of the evidence on which this statement is based comes from a few unprepossessing sites near the little fishing village of Ocós, fronting the Pacific only a few miles inside the Guatemala border. To the recent arrival, this is just one more, unbearably hot, tropical coast, with no conspicuous ancient ruins to entice the traveler to linger. To an ecology-minded archaeologist, however, this is a place of great fascination, for here we have not one kind of natural surroundings, but many.

The most obvious of these microenvironments is the beach itself, pounded by the Pacific surf, but affording to ancient and modern peoples with sufficient patience a number of

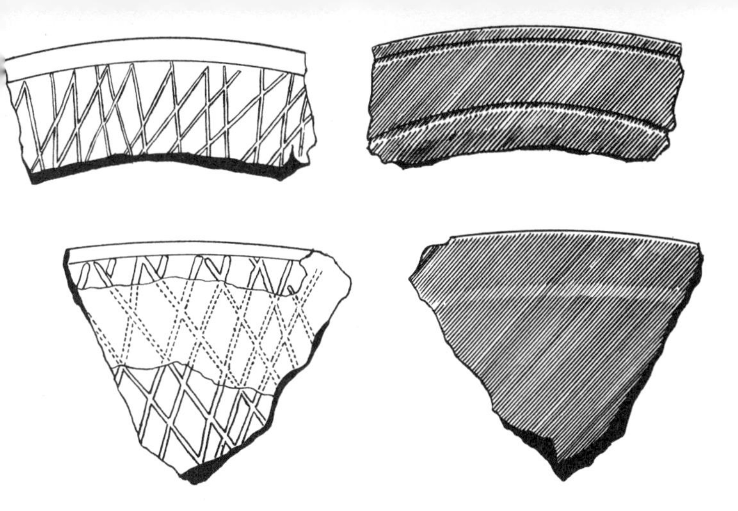

small, edible, burrowing crabs. Two rivers, the Naranjo and Suchiate, empty into the sea near Ocós; just in back of the barrier beach they connect with a complex set of lagoons. Today, the fishing is spectacularly good in the river mouth and estuary system, with snook, porgy, snapper, and other food fish caught by hand lines, gill nets, and circular throw nets; this is designated Microenvironment No. 2. Microenvironment No. 3 would be the so-called mangrove "swamps" that fringe the lagoons and estuaries.

Far from being the inhospitable barrier to travel pictured in many books, the mangrove forests and their muddy floors are a rich source of wild foods: the mollusks that can be dug from the mud, the oysters and mussels that cling to the roots of the mangroves, the land crabs that scurry about on the flats. Slightly farther inland are other microenvironments—the rivers themselves, the annually flooded patches of tropical savanna, and the most important of them all, the higher ground covered with tropical forest.

Here, then, is an ecologically complex environment that would have offered a good life to a nonagricultural people. Here on the Pacific Coast these microenvironments were close enough to each other that all could be exploited from a single settlement. Add farming to this, and what would one have? Considering that the better-drained soils, once cleared of their towering forest cover, are so fertile that two or three crops can be produced in a single year without rotation, the implications for sedentism are obvious. A greater contrast with the limited possibilities of the arid Tehuacán environment could hardly be imagined.

We have dug ancient settlements here that throw light on these conditions. Typical of these sites would be La Victoria, which an earlier generation of archaeologists would never have looked at. It is located on a now filled-in estuary (detectable on aerial photographs) and made up of about a dozen low earthen mounds that once supported pole-and-thatch houses with walls daubed with clay. In the deepest levels reached at La Victoria in 1958, we hit upon the Ocós culture, one of the oldest ever found in the region.

It is estimated to begin by 1300 B.C. Ocós has extremely sophisticated pottery that emphasizes just those shapes which were favored by the Abejas and Purrón people of Tehuacán, and is often decorated with a strange, coppery, iridescent slip or by impressing the wet clay with cord-wrapped paddles or the edges of shells. Dozens of fragments from little, hand-modeled figurines of fired clay were found; if we had dug all of La Victoria, we probably should have come up with thousands. All seem to represent women. Were they made for some cult of fertility? Or for children's dolls? We have as yet no answer, but from this time on they were to become a hallmark for almost all Formative cultures in Mesoamerica.

Unluckily, all perishable food remains had in fact perished in the Ocós debris. But animal bones were found that indicated a little hunting, and we know that they had the domestic dog. Most of the faunal remains, however, came from turtles, and there were quantities

Everywhere in Formative stage villages in Mesoamerica clay figurines of women were fashioned in great number. Why there was such a prevailing preoccupation with the female form is still unknown, though some archaeologists believe they may have been fertility symbols. The idea of making such figures may have come from the Pacific Coast of Ecuador, where similar objects from a far earlier time have been found. At right are figurines from the Ocós phase at La Victoria.

of oyster and mussel shells. Significantly, these indicated a people less interested in hunting than in collecting the wild food resources *immediately* at hand, that is, from the mangrove-lined estuary lying right at their doorsteps. We have no direct evidence that the Ocós people farmed, but metates (flat grinding stones) and manos (cylindrical hand stones) showed that they were probably milling corn, perhaps to make tamales.

Just across the Naranjo River, a few miles to the east of La Victoria, the even smaller site of Salinas La Blanca produced an early Formative culture (Cuadros), which followed Ocós in time. Here we had one of those lucky situations that practically never occur in the tropical lowlands—the almost miraculous preservation of vegetable foodstuffs, through impregnation by carbonates contained in the soil. We were able to reconstruct with confidence the way of life of an Indian people on the Guatemala coast between 1100 and 850 B.C. Here was a completely sedentary hamlet. The scanty animal bones showed that hunting was of no importance. Far more abundant were fish bones, pieces of turtle carapace, and fragments of crab claws known to come from a species living in the mangroves. All of the mollusks found could have been scooped from the mangrove mud.

But these people were also farmers, and here we had unmistakable evidence: a large number of "fossilized" corncobs, which Mangelsdorf was able to identify as belonging to a primitive race known as early as 3000 B.C. in Archaic sites of the Tehuacán Valley. Of the many thousands of pottery fragments dug up at Salinas La Blanca, more than 90 per cent were from a kind of large, neckless, globular jar that was doubtless used for the cooking of corn dough in some form, most likely as tamales.

The significance of the Cuadros culture is that it represents a mode of existence that was unknown then or previously at Tehuacán. Here was a settlement placed among a number of microenvironments or small ecological niches, but the Cuadros people exploited the food resources of only three of these: the mangrove forests, the river and its banks, and the cultivatable fields just in back of the site. At no time in the year did they have to pack their belongings and move to a more distant niche because of depletion or disappearance of food resources close at hand.

This is the real difference between the seminomadic highland Indians of the Archaic stage and the early Formative peoples of the Mesoamerican lowlands. We believe that the lowlanders were already semisettled before the arrival of agriculture, that the richly endowed littoral gave them abundant food supplies almost the year round. We also think that at some time between 2000 and 1500 B.C. domestic corn and perhaps other plants were taken down the great river systems (such as the Papaloápan, which reaches from the Tehuacán Valley to the Gulf Coast), and that it was this additional energy source that produced in the Veracruz and Chiapas-Guatemala lowlands the second great transition of Mesoamerican life: the achievement of the Formative stage, with full sedentism.

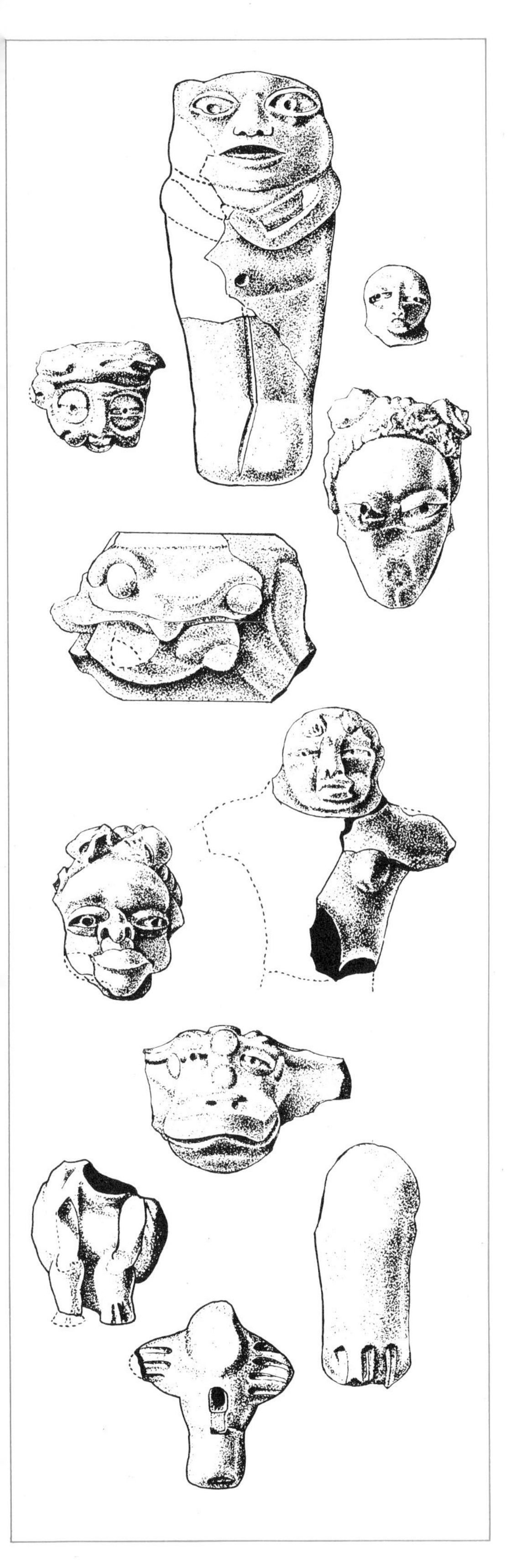

Once established, the Formative way of life, which is in every sense the counterpart of the Neolithic in the Old World, spread throughout much of Mexico and Central America. It took root early in the Valley of Mexico, where the reedy shores of the great lake abounded in wild fowl, and its waters in fish.

It was the simple female figurines of pottery found in these Formative villages near Mexico City that Gamio had seen as evidence for a pre-Teotihuacán culture then called Archaic. In fact, there is hardly any part of Mesoamerica that was not densely occupied within the Formative span (1500 B.C.–A.D. 200). But, as shall be seen, the very simplicity of these early cultures, with their thatch-roofed villages, modestly decorated pottery, amusing little figurines, and so forth, has been deceptive, for at one time it was thought that the great Classic civilizations had sprung, like Athena from the brow of Zeus, directly from such a milieu. That is, the hypothetical sequence would have been: a postulated prepottery stage, now known to have existed (the Archaic); the Formative stage, then known only as an epoch of village life, with perhaps the addition of some ceremonialism and even small pyramids toward its close (*ca.* A.D. 200–300); and the great Classic cultures like Teotihuacán and the Maya. The picture is one of smooth progress, as food resources and populations expanded, toward an increasingly complex life.

The facts and concepts on which this "steady evolution" picture has been built have been seriously shaken by the discovery of the Olmec civilization.

3. THE OLMEC REVEALED

In 1869 there appeared a brief notice, signed "J. M. Melgar," in the bulletin of the Mexican Society of Geography and Statistics, part of which translates as follows:

In 1862 I was in the region of San Andres Tuxtla, a town of the state of Veracruz, in Mexico. During my excursions, I learned that a Colossal Head had been unearthed a few years before, in the following manner. Some one-and-a-half leagues from a sugar-cane hacienda, on the western slopes of the Sierra of San Martín, a laborer of this hacienda, while cutting the forest for his field, discovered on the surface of the ground what looked like the bottom of a great iron kettle turned upside down. He notified the owner of the hacienda, who ordered its excavation. And in place of the kettle was discovered the above-mentioned head. It was left in the excavation as one would not think to move it, being of granite and measuring two yards in height with corresponding proportions. . . . On my arrival at the hacienda I asked the owner to take me to look at it. We went, and I was struck with surprise: as a work of art, it is without exaggeration a magnificent sculpture . . . but what astonished me was the Ethiopic type represented. I reflected that there had undoubtedly been Negroes in this country, and that this had been in the first epoch of the world.

The article was accompanied by an engraving of what we now know as Monument A at Tres Zapotes. So struck was Melgar by his theory of Negro voyages from Africa to Mexico that he took up his pen again in 1871 for further wild speculations, quite in line with

The largest known Colossal Head, from San Lorenzo, was discovered in 1946.

The first modern archaeologist to explore the Olmec sites of southeastern Mexico was Frans Blom (below, right), a native of Denmark, who, along with the American writer and anthropologist Oliver La Farge (left), journeyed through the lowland jungles of Veracruz and Tabasco in 1925. Despite their pioneering work, Blom and La Farge remained convinced that they had encountered not a separate and older civilization, but only the marginal remains of the Maya.

the migrationist theories of his time. To him, however, belongs the distinction of being the first to publish an object—remarkable enough in its own right—belonging to what we now know as the Olmec civilization.

One would think that the presence of a colossal stone head (of basalt, not granite) measuring over six feet high would have attracted further notice to the archaeological resources of the southern Gulf Coast. Instead, there was only silence, broken in 1905 by the visit of the German archaeologist Eduard Seler and his wife to the head. But the head's true significance remained unappreciated for many years more.

We next turn to one of the great pioneer archaeologist-explorers of Mesoamerica. Frans Blom, born in Denmark in 1893, first came to Mexico as a young man in the employ of one of the many foreign oil companies then drilling along the Gulf Coast lowlands. Captivated by the ruins that he encountered there, he began a long career as a discoverer of the Mesoamerican past. In those days, Tulane University in New Orleans had just started exploring the Mesoamerican field, and Blom was put in charge of a two-man expedition to explore the wild country of southern Mexico and neighboring Guatemala, an area then almost totally unknown to the scholarly world.

In February of 1925, Blom, accompanied by the young anthropologist Oliver La Farge (later to be better known for his Pulitzer Prize novel, *Laughing Boy*, and for his political and cultural activities in behalf of the American Indian), left New Orleans for the south. These were the days before insecticides and antibiotics had been invented, and it was no light matter to make such journeys as theirs proved to be. Proceeding overland along the Veracruz coast, and incidentally being the first to report the monument on the volcano of San Martín Pajápan (a stone now known to be Olmec), they left the wretched port of Coatzacoalcos by motor sloop for the mouth of the Tonalá River, in westernmost Tabasco. In the steady company of bloodthirsty mosquitoes, they made their way up the river and into a tributary stream, finally arriving at the swamp-bound island of La Venta, about which they had heard local reports.

Blom and La Farge thus discovered La Venta, the greatest Olmec archaeological site, with its multitude of great stone sculptures. One of these was another Colossal Head, which they immediately related to the one in Tres Zapotes reported by the Selers. But it was not for them to realize the true significance of their findings, namely, that they had found the oldest New World civilization. On the contrary, the final comment of these two great explorers was that "we are inclined to ascribe these ruins to the Maya culture"! Nonetheless, the account of La Venta that they published in their scholarly and entertaining *Tribes and Temples* gave a great impetus to Olmec research.

It was at this time that the name "Olmec" or "Olmeca" began to creep into the literature on the archaeology of this little-known region. The term had been around for a long time. Traditionally, going back as far as the sixteenth-century accounts of Father Sahagún and the native chroniclers, it had referred to

the people of the southern Gulf Coast, situated between the Totonac Indians to the north and the Xicalanca Maya situated to the east, in Tabasco. Derived from the Náhuatl (Aztec) root *ollin*, meaning "rubber," Olmec may be translated as "the rubber people," that is, people from the lands where rubber is produced. These historic Olmec had wandered far, and in late pre-Hispanic times were definitely involved in political events in the highlands of central Mexico.

To one German and two American archaeologists go not only the credit for recognizing an entirely new civilization in southern Veracruz and Tabasco, but also the blame for the sin of fixing the term "Olmec" to it. This was a mistake as bad in its way as calling the British ruins of Stonehenge "Druidic," for we now know that the Druids were Celtic priests who lived many centuries after that great circular temple had fallen into ruin. The first of these scholars was Hermann Beyer, who in a 1927 review of *Tribes and Temples* saw the similarity between a small stone carving formerly in his possession and the strange monument encountered by Blom and La Farge at the top of San Martín Pajápan volcano, and proposed that both be ascribed to the "Olmec or Totonac civilization." Next was Marshall Saville, head of the Museum of the American Indian in New York City. In a monograph put out by the museum in 1929, Saville compared the San Martín sculpture with several strange "votive" axes and a number of small jade objects from museum collections, and he realized that all were in the same, strange art style, one that emphasized a creature with slanting oval eyes, thick lips and snarling mouth, and a cleft over the forehead. Since it was hardly likely that the San Martín monolith had been moved very far, he said that it was in southern Veracruz that this art style had been produced, by a culture that he, also, called "Olmec."

Finally, we come to the contribution of George C. Vaillant. American archaeology has had few practitioners more brilliant than this Harvard graduate whose interest was early drawn to Mexico. In 1928 he began excavating ancient villages in the Valley of Mexico belonging to the pre-Classic, Formative stage—village remains that he knew could not represent the beginnings of aboriginal life here and for which he therefore applied the name "Middle Cultures." Vaillant was then a curator at the American Museum of Natural History in New York, into whose Mexican collection came a lovely little jade carving of a crouching beast with part-human, part-jaguar characteristics, which has become known as a werejaguar. Like his colleague Saville, Vaillant recognized the affinity of the strange, almost Oriental style in which this piece was fashioned with the huge sculptures that had been published by Blom and La Farge. His 1932 paper on the subject again applied the name "Olmec" to the new civilization. And so it has stuck—as difficult to shake off as a childhood nickname—inaccurate and misleading, to the great early culture of southern Veracruz and Tabasco. Several attempts have been made over the last thirty years to change it to something more fitting, but neither professionals nor public have ever

That Olmec remains all have a strong similarity in style, and so suggest the existence of a major, independent culture, was first recognized by George Vaillant, an American archaeologist. His definition of Olmec civilization, as a unified cultural phase, resulted from work he carried on in the 1920's and 1930's. While others had used the name Olmec, Vaillant made it stick. What the Olmec may have called themselves will probably never be known.

accepted any appellation other than "Olmec."

By about 1938 there were strongly grounded suspicions that an entirely new civilization, somehow related to the Maya but different from it, and of an unknown age, was to be discovered in the jungle strongholds of the southern Gulf Coast plain. The man who actually made the discovery was Matthew W. Stirling, who has played the same part for the Olmec as Stephens had done a century earlier for the ancient Maya. Archaeological "discovery" on a big scale means more than an armchair excursion, no matter how brilliant, into the past. It means years of hard work, of on-the-ground exploration, and of patient excavation. The kind of man who can find an ancient civilization must be multifaceted. A capability for hard work; a good physique; a resistance to biting insects, diseases, and all the other hardships of life in the field before insecticides and other modern refinements came on the market; a good education and wide reading in the related literature; and, most important of all, a great deal of intuition, of being able to see relationships between things that others have generally not seen, and of playing such hunches right: all of these go into the make-up of the great pioneer archaeologist. It also helps to have the courage of one's convictions in order to weather the storms of criticism that such finds are likely to stir up, as in the case of Schliemann at Troy or of Sir Arthur Evans, the discoverer of Minoan civilization on Crete.

Stirling began to be intrigued by the possible existence of an entirely new civilization as far back as 1918, when, as a student at the University of California, he came across a picture of a "crying baby" maskette of jade owned by the Berlin Museum. After joining the staff of the Smithsonian Institution he continued this interest, much struck by the circumstance that objects in the same style were usually of a bluish jade, a kind of stone not found among the other Mesoamerican civilizations. With much excitement he read the report by Blom and La Farge on La Venta, as well as an account of the first Colossal Head and other monuments at Tres Zapotes (then called Hueyapán) brought out in 1932 by Albert Weyerstall, an American planter in Veracruz. Incidentally, while describing a monument taken from La Venta to the schoolhouse in Villahermosa, Tabasco, Weyerstall had this to say:

Once while questioning an American archaeologist about this particular idol, the writer was informed that it (as well as those still remaining at La Venta) was decidedly not Maya, but pre-Maya—therefore about three thousand years old.

One can only wonder: Who was this remark able prophet? For this was the only suggestion ever made prior to Stirling's excavations at La Venta regarding its great antiquity, and it was an extremely close approximation of its true age!

In early 1938 Stirling took the earliest opportunity to visit Melgar's Colossal Head. This was no easy trip then, for the network of paved roads that now crisscrosses almost all regions of Mexico was hardly existent. After an eight-hour ride on horseback from the picturesque town of Tlacotálpan, to which it is possible to

It was on jade objects such as these (from the American Museum of Natural History) that Vaillant based his definition of the Olmec style. Both the Kunz ax at left and the small figurine at right represent the Rain God, which the Olmec conceived of as part jaguar, part "crying baby." By comparing these and other objects with remains being recovered along Mexico's lower Gulf Coast, Vaillant was able to deduce the possible homeland of the newly discovered civilization.

journey by boat, he arrived at the hacienda of Hueyapán on the southwestern slopes of the Tuxtla Mountains. It was on the former lands of this estate that the head had been reported to lie, but Stirling soon discovered that it was to be found only a mile or so from the little village of Tres Zapotes. Impressed as he was by his first view of the head, he was amazed by the number of great earthen mounds, one almost 450 feet long, in its vicinity. Clearly this was an archaeological site of tremendous importance, and Stirling was able to enlist, upon his return to Washington, the support of the National Geographic Society and the Smithsonian Institution for a massive program of excavation at Tres Zapotes. It was the first such enterprise of any scope ever to be entered upon in southern Veracruz.

So back he came the following January by the same route, this time with a completely equipped expedition. All supplies had to be taken up the Papaloápan River to Tlacotálpan, then by another launch journey up the winding river system until a tiny hamlet was reached, from which it was possible to bring in, on muleback, all personnel, supplies, and the expedition director to Tres Zapotes. Only those who have experienced the difficulties of supplying a large-scale operation under such rugged conditions can appreciate the achievement of archaeologists in the pre-Jeep, pre-airstrip era.

Two long field seasons, in 1939 and 1940, were spent at Tres Zapotes. In one of those ironic acts of fate that are very common on digs, the greatest find ever made there was stumbled across in the first few days after the arrival of the Stirling group. In front of a large mound within one of the principal groups at the site, the corner of a worked piece of basalt projected a few inches above the ground. It looked enough like a buried monument to Stirling, who had been shown it by one of the local farmers, to warrant excavation. Within a short time it was clear that this was a broken stela (flat, carved, or inscribed stone of rectangular shape) that had been set upright in ancient times behind a flat stone altar, recalling the stela-altar complex so common in the Classic Maya centers. This was no ordinary stela, however, for this monument, now called Stela C, proved to have an inscription on one face, and an Olmec-like werejaguar mask on the other.

Stirling immediately recognized the inscription as a date in the Long Count system used by the Classic Maya. A set of elegantly carved bar-and-dot numbers was arranged in a vertical row. The Maya were able to get along with a combination of only three symbols to write any numeral: a bar for five, a dot for one, and a stylized shell for zero. Four was expressed by four dots, six by a bar and a dot, and ten by two bars. For twenty and higher numbers, positional numeration was used, but this was not needed for Maya dates, which never had coefficients above this figure. Briefly, the Long Count consists of a tabulation of days elapsed since the supposed inception of the calendar, the total being expressed as so many cycles of differing magnitudes. The largest of these cycles is the *baktun*, containing 144,000 days; the next, the *katun*, 7,200 days; then the *tun*, with 360 days; the *uinal*, with 20; and the

More than any other archaeologist, Matthew Stirling of the Smithsonian Institution was the real discoverer of the Olmec. Stirling's first major work in Olmec country was at Tres Zapotes in 1939. He is shown (in that year) measuring a Colossal Head. Subsequent expeditions took him to the most important of all Olmec sites, La Venta and San Lorenzo. From the first, Stirling was convinced that Olmec civilization predated every other known in Mesoamerica.

OVERLEAF: *A view of Monument 17, the most recent Colossal Head found at San Lorenzo, shows the overgrown jungle environment where Olmec archaeologists work. Carved from basalt, by sculptors who had no metal tools, heads such as this one weigh approximately 18 tons. Each head is believed to be a portrait of a real Olmec king, and the characteristic headgear may represent a helmet worn during a ball game, which has been shown to have had ceremonial importance.*

smallest of all, always at the bottom of the column, the *kin* of one day. Each of these in the days of Maya ascendancy was shown with its own hieroglyph, while to its left stood the coefficient by which it was to be multiplied.

Stela C resembled the Tuxtla statuette (a duck-billed figure of jade inscribed with a very early Long Count date, found long ago in Veracruz) in that the cycle glyphs were not given, only the coefficients. Although the baktun number was broken off at the top of the stone, Stirling was able to do some quick calculation to arrive at a reconstruction of the whole date. This was (in the form that Long Count dates are usually written) 7.16.6.16.18, arriving at a day 6 Eznab in their ritual "almanac year" of 260 days. Using J. Eric Thompson's correlation of Maya and Christian calendars, this was the equivalent of a day in the year 31 B.C. Not only was this earlier than the Tuxtla statuette, but it was some 330 years older than the beginning of the Classic Maya civilization. Now the fat was in the fire—here was an Olmec-appearing monument with an inscription in the so-called Maya system that was found far west of the Maya area itself. The immediate implication to Stirling was that Olmec civilization was older than Maya, and that at least the calendrical aspect of Maya culture had, in fact, been invented by the Olmec.

Stirling was not alone in this opinion. George Vaillant had also reached the same conclusion, for in his surely pre-Classic site of Gualupita, just outside the town of Cuernavaca in highland Mexico, he had excavated hollow pottery figures of the purest Olmec style. But even more important was the growing body of opinion favoring Olmec priority in these matters among several influential Mexican archaeologists. Among these was Alfonso Caso, who had begun the mammoth task of excavating and restoring the huge archaeological center of Monte Albán in Oaxaca as far back as 1931. He, like Vaillant, was finding that the Olmec art style, with its unmistakable characteristics, had penetrated here as long ago as Monte Albán I, long before the Classic stage. Another was the late Miguel Covarrubias. By profession an artist, Covarrubias' enormous intellect and tremendous enthusiasm had early expanded to take in the field of Mexican archaeology and anthropology. No other person could rival him in his intuition about the Mesoamerican past and in his feeling for objects and styles. As much collector as archaeologist, he had acquired Olmec pieces from both the Gulf Coast and the highlands; moreover, he had participated in many archaeological digs. It was not long before Covarrubias began proclaiming, like Caso, that Olmec was the "mother culture" of Mesoamerica. To this group of scholars Stela C came as confirmation. It can well be imagined that there was a spirited opposition from entrenched Maya scholars.

This was not all they found at Tres Zapotes. Several other monuments had been seen, like the first Colossal Head, by previous travelers, such as a four-foot-long stone "box," quite fragmentary, which was carved on its four sides with strange scenes of a battle taking place before swirling clouds. This, and others at the site, are, however, not really Olmec but in a

later style—important enough in its own right—which we shall call Izapan. On the other hand, some were fully Olmec. The implication is that more than one civilization occupied Tres Zapotes. This is more than confirmed by the thousands of fragments of pottery and figurines disgorged by the Tres Zapotes earth during the two field seasons of 1939 and 1940: there are probably no less than five phases or cultures represented, extending from Olmec times right up through the Spanish conquest. The stratigraphic situation is so confusing that we shall turn to other Olmec sites to find exactly what happened during the Olmec apogee.

Stirling's next move was obvious: to go to La Venta. This turned out to be the most magnificent Olmec site ever dug, for it is the key to Olmec culture. It is La Venta, for instance, that has provided the first radiocarbon dates run on Olmec material, dates which are far earlier than anyone would have guessed in the years from 1939 to 1943, when Stirling's great discoveries at the Olmec metropolis followed in rapid succession. If its true time position had then been known, it is likely that a great deal of controversy would have been hushed.

Because of the considerable excitement generated by Stirling's finds among Mexican and American archaeologists, the Mexican Society of Anthropology called a round-table conference on the subject in July, 1941. There was general accord among those present—who included Caso, Covarrubias, and Stirling—that the Olmec culture (which they preferred to call "La Venta") was the first high civilization of Mexico. But in that same month a bombshell had been prepared and published, under the innocuous title, "Dating of Certain Inscriptions of Non-Maya Origin." This was by Eric Thompson, the outstanding Maya scholar of his day and the leading expert on Maya hieroglyphs.

This was an enormously erudite paper that set out to prove several things at once. First, that all of the non-Maya inscriptions from the Olmec area, with their seemingly early dates, were in fact late. And second, that the archaeological Olmec were no earlier than A.D. 1200, contemporary with the Toltec of Mexico and Yucatán. Thompson's attack on the Olmec enthusiasts sounds like a minority view, but in actuality it was shared by most American archaeologists working in Mesoamerica at the time. It was Stirling who was very much in the minority party. The famous Mayanist Sylvanus G. Morley was also of Thompson's opinion. Indeed, the whole Maya field was up in arms—what civilization could possibly be more ancient than that of their beloved Maya?

The trouble was that Thompson, with his vast learning, was a very hard man to refute. Caso, Covarrubias, and Stirling had the necessary tenacity, but they could not shake what seemed like the soundest kind of scholarship, and there were very few archaeologists before 1957 who would have cared to go against the Maya experts and place the Olmec before A.D. 300, that is, in the pre-Classic era. In that year, however, a second bombshell came along: the new radiocarbon dates on La Venta. These ranged from 1160 to 580 B.C.

Stirling had been vindicated: this truly was Mesoamerica's first civilization.

The most exciting discovery made by Stirling at Tres Zapotes was Stela C (below, right), a fragmentary rock slab with a date carved in the Maya calendrical system, known as the Long Count. The date corresponds with 31 B.C., which is three centuries earlier than the oldest known Maya inscription. On the reverse side is carved a Late Olmec mask of the Rain God. Stela C was conclusive proof that the Olmec predated the Maya. In the Late Olmec and Maya systems only three symbols were needed to write any number. A stylized shell signified zero, a dot represented one, and a bar, five (depicted below). For twenty and higher numbers, positional numeration was used. The best known and most beautiful of the Maya codices, an astronomical and ritual almanac dating from about the 12th century A.D., is below at left. It represents the mathematical and astronomical culmination begun by the Olmec.

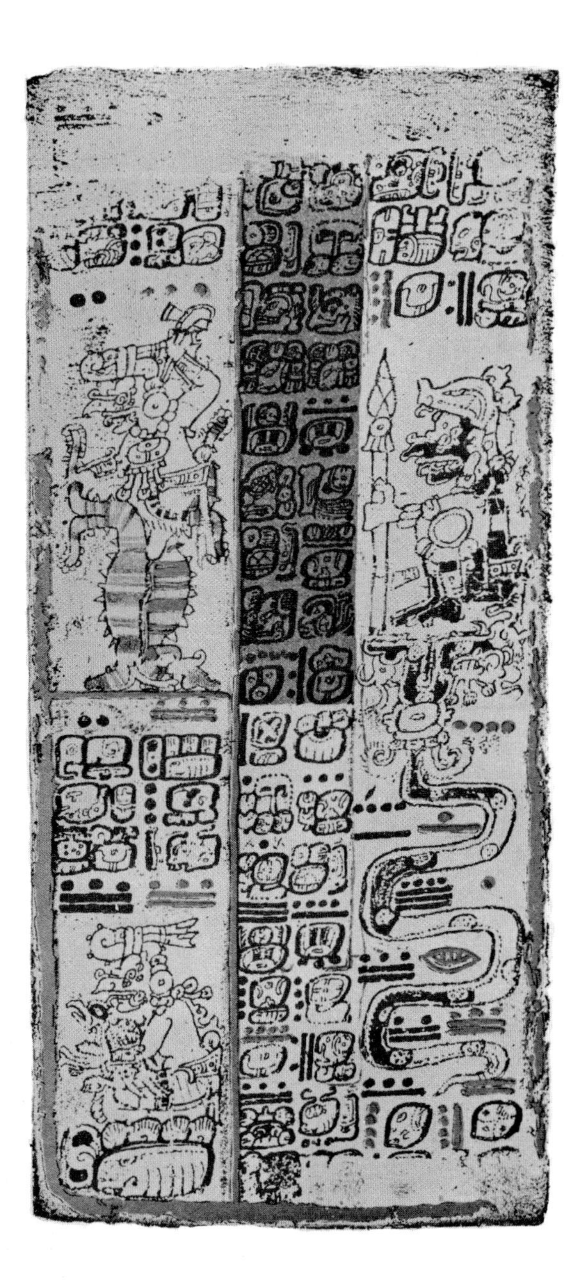

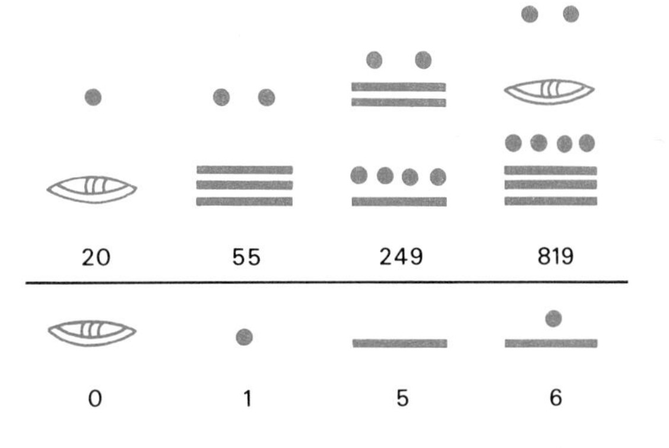

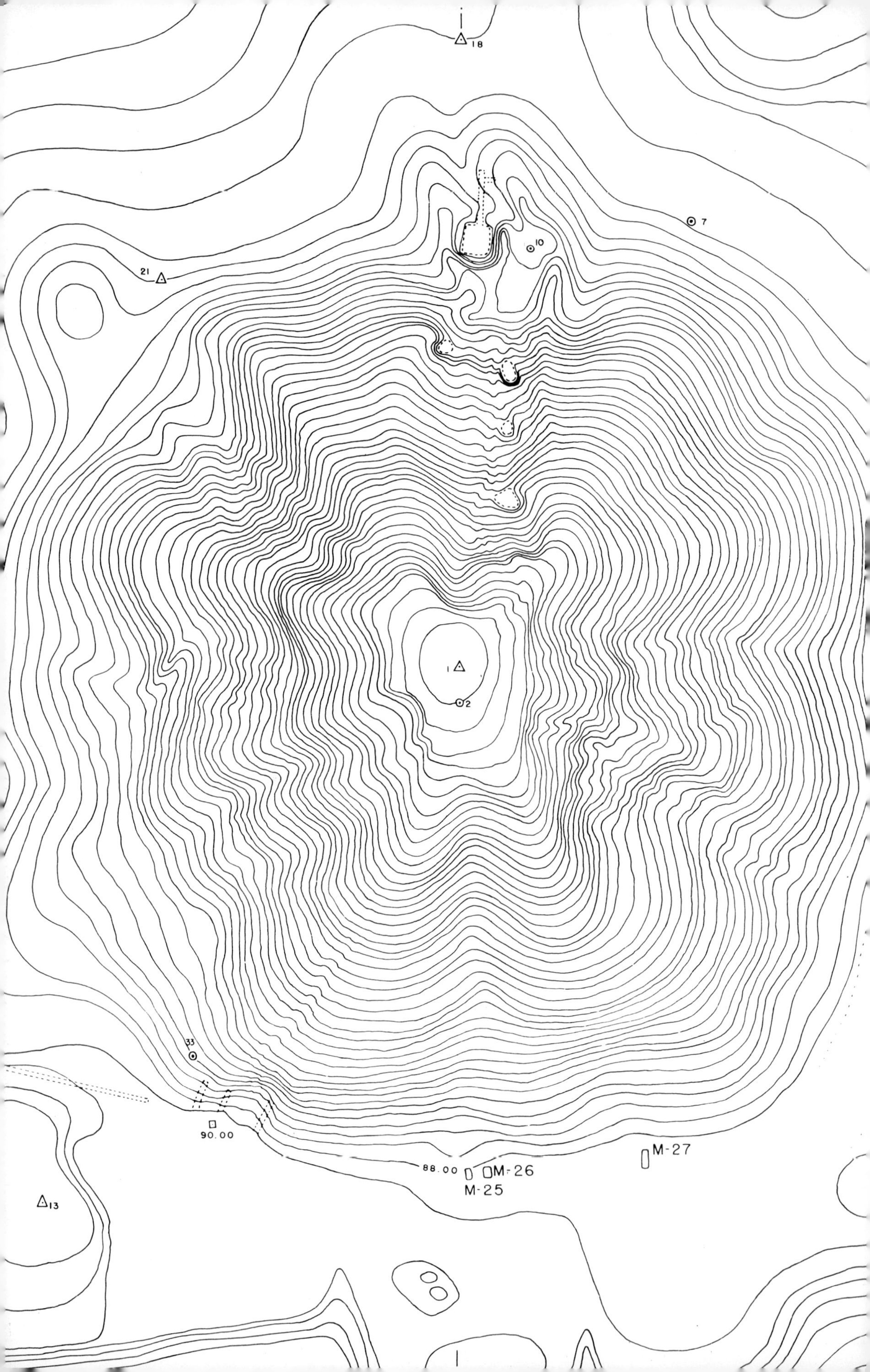
18
7
10
21
1
2
33
90.00
88.00
M-26
M-25
M-27
13

4. LA VENTA: SANCTUARY IN THE SWAMPS

The laborious passage to La Venta from the Veracruz port of Coatzacoalcos undertaken by Blom and La Farge over forty years ago is now a matter of a half-hour drive over a paved highway. But we need not pity the explorers of yesterday, for La Venta, the glory of the ancient Olmec, has lately changed very much for the worse. In place of the luxurious tropical vegetation that once covered the place, and the simple life then followed by its peasants, there are now all the horrors of modern industrial civilization. An oil refinery belches fumes, an airstrip bisects the archaeological site, and gas flares light up the night sky across the waste-clogged swamps. La Venta has fallen victim to the oil under its surface and is dying in its own black blood.

But let us forget the present and go back to the site as it looked when Stirling first laid eyes upon it. La Venta is, or was, an island set in the marshes lying east of the sluggish Tonalá River, which divides the states of Veracruz and Tabasco as it flows north to the Gulf of Mexico. It is likely that the Tonalá once bordered on the island itself, for according to the oil geologists, La Venta is being pushed up—at an almost imperceptible rate—by a deeply buried salt dome, a relic of the shallow sea that covered the southern Gulf Coast plains several million years ago. As the island rose, the ancient river was divided and flowed around it (this might well have been the situation during Olmec times). As the salt dome continued to ascend, the Tonalá was displaced to its present course some three miles to the west.

A dozen miles to the north of La Venta lie

A recent topographical map reveals the true shape of the great La Venta "pyramid."

The core of the Olmec heartland is comprised of three chief sites: Tres Zapotes, La Venta, and San Lorenzo. Perhaps not surprisingly, these sites, set among meandering lowland rivers in a forbidding tangle of swamps, grasslands, and forests, had been largely bypassed by archaeologists until relatively recent times. But here, from 1939 to 1946, Matthew Stirling began the work that, aided by the endeavors of later archaeologists, was to result in the unveiling of the Olmec.

the beaches of the Gulf Coast, frequently pounded by fierce *nortes* (northers that sweep down from Texas and northern Mexico in the wintertime, lashing Veracruz and Tabasco with cold rains). These nortes carry sand scoured from the great lines of beach dunes south, as far as La Venta itself. There is a saying along the Gulf Coast, "*Cuando no hay norte, hay sur*" (When there is no norther, there is a south wind). The southers, hot and as dry as any mistral out of Africa, blow up from the Pacific side of the Isthmus of Tehuantepec during April and May, bringing to the Olmec region its only true dry season. Torrential, monsoon-like rains begin at the end of May and last through November. Then the norte season begins again. Small wonder that archaeologists tended to avoid Olmec country like the plague.

But Matthew Stirling was an exception. His first trip to La Venta took place in 1940, after the Tres Zapotes excavations. The Stirling party proceeded east from Coatzacoalcos over dirt roads, then by launch up the mangrove-bordered Tonalá River until they reached the mouth of the Blasillo, a tributary from which it was possible to reach La Venta by foot or on muleback. At the juncture of the two rivers, by pure accident, they came upon the camp of one of the first oil geologists to prospect in the region; unluckily for Mexico's past, he found what he was looking for.

Back in those days, La Venta was a sort of tropical paradise, presided over by an eighty-year-old Indian, Don Sebastián Torres, who had come to this spot fifty years before, and with his small family had cut down the tall jungle and had wrested from it a modest living as a corn farmer. The Torres family has survived, but there is little left of the peaceful island that Don Sebastián once knew.

Stirling and his wife were immediately invited to stay at the Torres settlement, and they began to hear about the mysterious stones that had been seen by Blom and La Farge. They were also told that on fine nights the ghosts of the Aztec emperor Moctezuma and his court were supposed to dance and sing in the ruins! The loneliness and danger experienced for so many years by the Torres family in their jungle fastness had certainly stimulated their imaginations. The dangers were not imaginary, however. One night during the Stirlings' stay that season, a large jaguar killed three of the family's hogs only two hundred yards from their house. Day after day Don Sebastián's son-in-law took Stirling to various stones that he knew, and Stirling saw for the first time the 100-foot-high "pyramid" that dominates La Venta—a monument subsequently proven to be one of the weirdest constructions known in the New World.

The monuments at La Venta turned out to be remarkable. In a very short time Stirling had seen the six stones described by Blom and La Farge, and a great many more. By the end of the 1940 season, no fewer than four Colossal Heads had been located and exposed, all similar to the great basalt head of Tres Zapotes, but each with a slightly different type of "football helmet" bearing its own distinctive ornament; Head No. 1, for instance, has a device shaped like a capital U that might be related to the

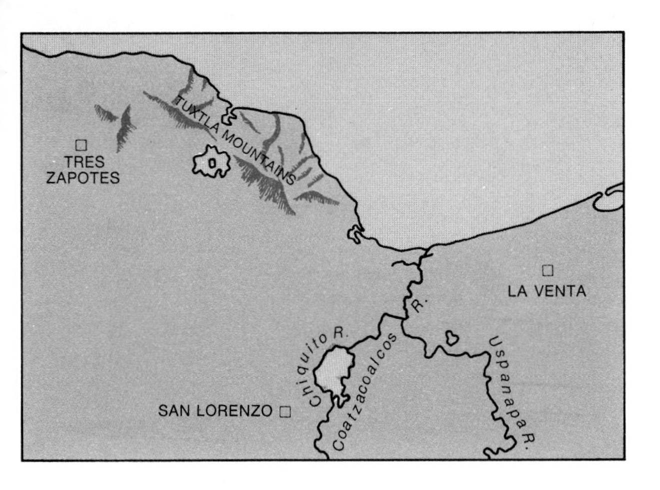

Maya moon glyph. Stirling presumed that all were portraits, and he was probably right. Even more outstanding than the heads were the "altars" of La Venta. The most exciting find was Altar 5, aptly termed the Quintuplet Altar. This enormous block of basalt had been carved on three sides. On its front, a richly garbed and mitered male personage emerges from an oven-like niche; he is seated cross-legged, and carries in his arms an infant—no ordinary child, but the cleft-headed, part-jaguar creature with snarling mouth, the very same creature that had been identified as the hallmark of the Olmec art style. On the sides of the altar were carved additional figures in relief: four adults with elaborate shoulder capes and headdresses, each holding a gesticulating, crying, werejaguar baby. What did this strange scene, so realistically and delicately carried out, really mean? Did we have here a king and his four wives, with the infants representing his own royal line of descent?

Needless to say, Stirling's early finds at La Venta aroused the greatest interest. One new monument was the most controversial of all. This was the great Stela 3, calculated by Stirling to weigh fifty tons, the largest of all the monuments ever found at La Venta. It measures no less than fourteen feet in height. On its front surface is a complex scene executed in relief with the same mastery as the Quintuplets. Two standing human figures with towering headdresses face each other, while above them float chubby little dwarfs whose features again recall the divine Olmec werejaguar. It is the face of the right-hand personage that is so curious, for here we do not have the flat-faced, almost Negroid visage of the Colossal Heads, but a goateed individual with a long, aquiline nose; among archaeologists, he quickly became known as Uncle Sam.

In the first place, the realism and complexity of the relief led opponents of Olmec priority to claim the monument as clearly contemporary with the Classic Maya. Secondly, the presence of Uncle Sam inspired Thor Heyerdahl, the Norwegian explorer and author of *Kon-Tiki*, among others, to claim a Nordic ancestry for at least some of the Olmec leadership. The first supposition was wrong, for Stela 3 is clearly Olmec and surely pre-Classic; as for the second, as we shall see, it is extremely misleading to use the testimony of artistic representations to prove ethnic theories. The Olmec were American Indians, not Negroes (as Melgar had thought) or Nordic supermen.

But it was while digging in front of Altar 1 (a huge monolith representing a cross-legged Olmec leader holding a rope leading to bound captives on both sides) that Stirling found what was a harbinger of the riches yet to come from La Venta's buried depths: jade. The Olmec were beyond any doubt the greatest craftsmen in the New World in the working of this extremely hard stone. It must be remembered that to all the Indians of Mesoamerica, jade was far and away the most precious substance known to them. A great ruler like the Emperor Moctezuma counted his riches not in gold (which was not known here until after A.D. 900) but in the precious green stone.

Now "jade" is a generic term. It is applied

Dominating the La Venta landscape is a 100-foot-high earth mound generally known as the Great Pyramid. It is the biggest structure ever built by the Olmec and may cover the tomb of a king. Only within the past few years have the shape and scale of the pyramid been revealed, as the jungle has been cleared to make way for a modern oil town. At right is one of the many La Venta monuments that depicts a recurring Olmec theme: a male figure cradling an infant Rain God.

not to one but to several different kinds of minerals, of which the two most important are nephrite and jadeite, both known to the jade workers of China. The peoples of Mesoamerica, including the Olmec, only knew the more precious jadeite. The word jade, in fact, was first applied to the green stones by the Spaniards in Mexico, who believed them to be effective in relieving kidney complaints and thus used the term *piedra de hijada* (stone of the kidney), later shortened to *jade.*

Until recently, the source of Mesoamerican jade was unknown. But in 1954, the late mineralogist William Foshag, acting on his knowledge that in nature jade is developed within formations of serpentine, suggested that jadeite pebbles and boulders ought to be found along the terraces of the Motagua River, which flows through serpentine hills in eastern Guatemala. This turned out to be the case. It is currently believed that the Classic Maya relied almost exclusively on this source for the exquisite jade used for plaques and other carvings which are found interred with their honored dead. But the best Maya jade is apple-green in color; only a fraction of Olmec jade is of this hue. The greatest Olmec pieces are, on the contrary, blue-green in color and quite translucent, while a few are of the transparent, dark green "jewel jade" so prized by the Chinese. Thus it appears that while the very ancient Olmec got some of their raw material from the Motagua, like the later Maya, there was some other source for the blue-green variety. Unfortunately, we still do not know where this was.

La Venta clearly cried out for a major archaeological effort, and the Smithsonian Institution decided to back it. The Stirling group returned in 1942, and, incidentally, with a great deal more comfort than previously, for the Mexican oil company Petroleos Mexicanos (PEMEX) had drilled a successful wildcat well in the vicinity and had made a camp at La Venta. They brought Dr. and Mrs. Stirling part way to La Venta by airplane. They had also run a canal connecting the island directly with the Tonalá River. The discovery of Olmec civilization at La Venta was therefore running a neck-and-neck race with the modern destruction of the site. Already settled on the island was Dr. Philip Drucker, a veteran of the Tres Zapotes dig. In addition to being an archaeologist, Drucker is one of the greatest experts on the Indians of the Northwest Coast (British Columbia and Alaska) and an adventurer of Hemingwayesque stature: he has at different times in his life been a cowboy, professional rodeo performer, an officer in the U.S. Navy, and a cattle rancher in the wilds of southern Veracruz. In 1942 and most subsequent seasons at La Venta, it was Drucker who provided the continuity, whatever the institution in charge.

The 1942 season was fantastically successful: two major tombs were found, unbelievably rich in jade offerings and other precious substances, each piece carved in the most sensitive and fully developed Olmec style. Stirling had little difficulty in persuading the National Geographic Society to back another expedition to La Venta in 1943; this time his assistant was Waldo Wedel of the Smithsonian, Drucker being on active wartime duty with the Navy.

The famous Stela 3 (left), found at La Venta, is calculated to weigh 50 tons and has a height of 14 feet, making it the largest Olmec carving yet unearthed. On its right side is a bearded, aquiline-nosed man (dubbed Uncle Sam by archaeologists), faced by a caped personage in towering headdress. Only a portion of the original remains, seen in the rendering below at left; it was defaced in ancient times for an unknown reason. Below at right is a hypothetical reconstruction.

Once more, there seemed to be no end to offerings and jade-stocked tombs; in addition, Wedel hit upon two of the great buried serpentine pavement masks that are among the most striking features of La Venta.

Let us recall exactly what the world of archaeology thought about the Olmec "problem" by this time. In 1941, the Mexicans—principally Alfonso Caso and Miguel Covarrubias—were proclaiming that the Olmec civilization of Veracruz and Tabasco was the "mother culture" of Mexico. Stirling thought that way too, for in a popular article of that year he said of the Olmec: "Their culture, which in many respects reached a high level, is very early and may well be the basic civilization out of which developed such high art centers as those of the Maya, Zapotecs, Toltecs [probably meaning Teotihuacán], and Totonacs."

But also remember that in 1941 Thompson published his famous paper, attempting to demolish that theory. The effect this had on American archaeology was profound, for by 1943 even Stirling had changed his mind about the age of Olmec civilization: "Their culture developed side by side with that of the Old Empire [i.e., Classic] Maya, but it differed widely in most aspects."

La Venta would then supposedly have been abandoned "between A.D. 500 and 800," according to Stirling. In subsequent years, interest in the Olmec subsided, except among the Mexicans. Covarrubias went on a kind of one man crusade for the Olmec, continuing to proclaim their immense antiquity—but this was mainly on the basis of his artistic intuition rather than upon any new data that had been provided by the 1941–1943 digs at La Venta.

By 1950, with the perfection of the radiocarbon system of dating, it was clearly time to take another look at the Olmec "problem." Who was right? In a major study of the Olmec brought out in 1952, Drucker himself leaned to a late date for La Venta, aligning it with the early Classic Maya (A.D. 300–600). But he was obviously not content with what was then known about the Olmec capital, for in 1955 he joined forces with Dr. Robert F. Heizer, a University of California archaeologist who is the leading authority on the prehistoric Indians of his state, for a massive investigation of the main ceremonial group at the site, again under the auspices of the Smithsonian and supported financially by the National Geographic Society. By this time enough was known of La Venta to enable them to concentrate their forces (fifty laborers working one hundred days) so as to get the most information in the shortest time. Most importantly, they knew that most of the offerings and tombs at La Venta were placed in relation to an imaginary line that bisects the site in a north-south direction. In the following year, the first radiocarbon dates for La Venta began to appear from the University of Michigan laboratory: between 800 and 400 B.C.

In subsequent years, Heizer and Drucker returned to La Venta several times. More radiocarbon samples were gathered, the earlier ones rechecked. La Venta is indeed ancient, and it is certainly as strange a site as ever was.

Because they dig a site from top to bottom, archaeologists usually work backward in time.

More than any other man who studied the Olmec, the late Miguel Covarrubias, a Mexican artist turned archaeologist, had an intense feeling for their art form and an intuitive conviction that they were indeed the "mother culture" of Mesoamerica. In many books and articles (written in English) and in his own drawings of Olmec sculpture (see pages 145–152) he did much to develop popular interest in the Olmec. The caricature at left is his view of himself as an Olmec.

Thus, the sequence of discovery is from the latest remains to the earliest, as a typical season (or series of seasons) progresses. We are going to turn this topsy-turvy world right side up, however, and describe what happened at La Venta as though we were writing a consecutive history for it.

We are now fairly sure that the first Olmec came to La Venta around 1100 years before Christ—as far back as the Early Formative. We can only guess from where they came. Presumably the island was then covered by a tall, tropical forest that they had to laboriously clear with stone axes and fire. These pioneers had a pretty clear idea of what they were to do: to construct a great temple center along a natural ridge running in a north-south direction in about the middle of the island. Leveling off the ridge by cutting and filling (just like any modern engineer), they seem to have begun the great clay "pyramid" that eventually was to reach a height of over one hundred feet, then a series of courts flanked by low mounds of specially selected colored clays to the north of it. This layout is not oriented to true north, but rather to a point 8° west of it. What did the orientation of the center line mean to the Olmec? We have no answer, but most scholars in this field think that an astronomical explanation must be sought—and adjusted for the night sky as it was three thousand years ago.

The next building phase might have taken place between 1000 and 800 B.C. and was marked by a stupendous display of organized work. The Olmec obviously believed in the principle of conspicuous waste when it came to expending labor and materials. Typical of this would be the features known as Massive Offerings. One of them was carried out in the following manner. First, an enormous pit representing the removal of fifteen thousand cubic feet of tough clay was dug down through a mound on the north of the Ceremonial Court, to a depth of sixteen feet. Then a course of serpentine blocks was placed on the bottom and the pit filled up again—but for what? Even more extraordinary were two other similar Massive Offerings. One such pit was fifty by sixty-one feet on a side and twenty-four feet deep; on its bottom had been placed over one thousand tons of serpentine slabs. The third such feature (put in during the next building phase) measured over seventy-seven feet on a side, was thirteen feet deep, and some sixty thousand cubic feet of material had been taken from it before the serpentine floor was laid in.

Even more mysterious are the three identical mosaic pavements that were set in place toward the end of this feverish period of construction. There are two on platforms flanking the south side of the Ceremonial Court and one just north of the Great Pyramid. Each consists of about 485 carefully shaped oblong blocks of serpentine covering an area of a little more than fifteen by twenty feet, set in colored clays. Although there has been some dispute about what the motif of the pavements is, the generally accepted idea is that it represents the mask of the Olmec werejaguar, highly conventionalized, with the typical cleft at the top of the head and diamond-shaped appendages below the face. The contrast of the green ser-

Digging below the surface of an adobe platform, the 1955 expedition (sponsored by the University of California, the Smithsonian, and the National Geographic Society) found one of the three pavement masks of La Venta. Each mask is a stylized face of the Olmec werejaguar (right) made up of nearly 500 blocks of serpentine. For all the artistry and labor that went into them, the masks were buried almost immediately after completion. Why, no one knows.

pentine with the yellow and orange sands that fill the features is indeed striking. Magnificent though they are to modern eyes, they also were destined to be Massive Offerings, for it appears that they were covered over almost as soon as they were finished. Lastly, on top of the clays that covered the mask of the Southeast Platform, the Olmec laid down an offering of twenty jade and serpentine celts (small stone axes) arranged as a kind of cross, with a concave mirror of hematite placed in the vertical bar of the "cross."

We shall come upon these concave mirrors again, for a number of them have been found at La Venta in offerings of slightly later date. These were made of some iron-rich ore that takes a high polish, such as hematite, ilmenite, or magnetite. The reflecting surfaces are concave, and it has been found that they had been ground, by a totally unknown process, to optical specifications, being just slightly parabolizing in curvature (the radius of curvature grows progressively greater as the edge is approached). They always have two perforations on one edge and thus could have been worn as chest ornaments; indeed, sculptured figures at La Venta and San Lorenzo—another great Olmec site—show that this was the case. But they must have had some use other than as ornaments. What could this have been? Experiments show that one can throw images of the outside world on a blank surface with them, and it is also sure that they can be used to start fires on a hot day. They must have given their owners, the Olmec rulers of La Venta, great ritual power and prestige.

On and on the site went after 800 B.C., probably being added to and dug into until its final abandonment, which, according to the most recent radiocarbon dates, must have been within the Middle Formative period, about 500 B.C. It was these two final building phases that saw the careful placement of some of the richest Olmec offerings at La Venta.

La Venta's greatest wealth and power were reached during its two final building phases. According to the most recent radiocarbon dates, this would have been after 800 B.C., but before its final abandonment, perhaps around 400 B.C. To this stage in the history of La Venta belong some of the finest offerings and burials ever found in the New World. Many of these are either placed exactly on the center line running through the site, or in relation to it, and the offerings themselves are often laid out so that their own long axis conforms with this center line orientation.

One of the very richest such deposits was Offering No. 2, found in 1955, which has no fewer than fifty-one polished celts, mostly of jade or serpentine. Five of them are finely engraved with typically Olmec designs. Once more, we are reminded of the incredible waste that the burial of these laboriously manufactured articles must represent. Why did they do it? For the gods? Or, more prosaically, as a display of the wealth that the Olmec leaders possessed?

Apparently in certain cases they knew where these offerings had been put. For this statement we have the testimony of the remarkable Offering No. 4. The goddess of archaeological

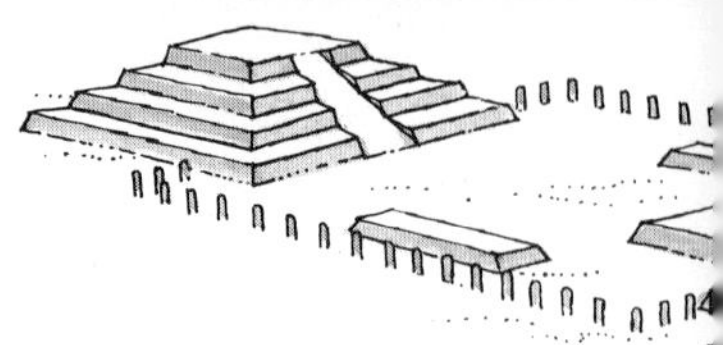

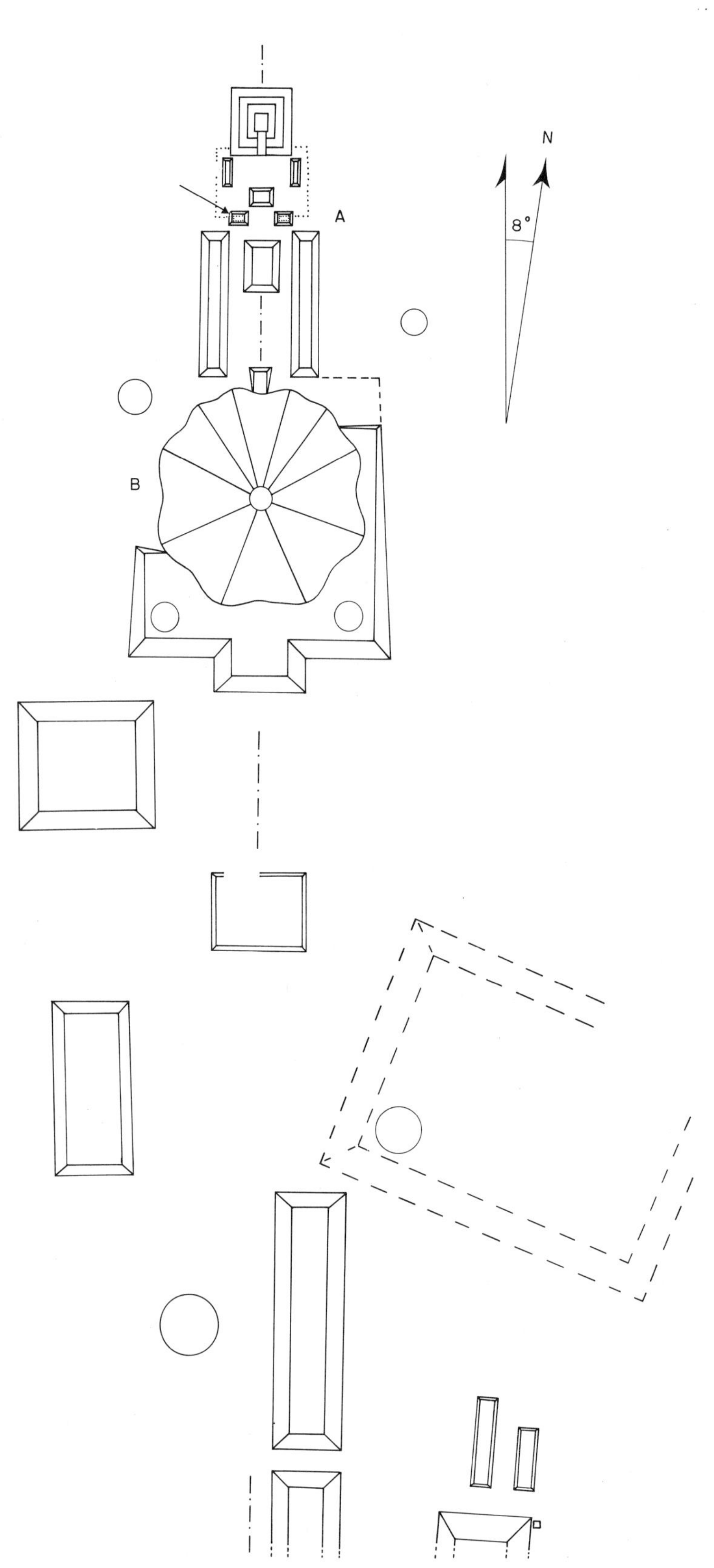

LA VENTA, *now recognized as the major ceremonial center of Olmec civilization, is built on a low ridge, on an island surrounded by swamps. The plan at left shows the most recent ideas on the size and organization of La Venta, with the Great Pyramid, now known to have been a fluted cone, as the focal point (B). Almost all the discoveries at the site (jade, tombs, pavement masks) have been made in the area north of the pyramid (A). The precise purpose of the area to the south is still not known, although several large Olmec monuments have been unearthed.*

The perspective drawing above shows what this area and the pyramid may have looked like. The color diagram is a cross section of a small platform just north of the pyramid (arrow at upper left of plan) and shows the extraordinary labors undertaken by the Olmec in entombing pavement masks. An enormous pit was dug down 24 feet. It was 50 feet wide, 61 feet long, and contained 1,000 tons of rough serpentine slabs. The pavement mask was placed at the top of the pit; the mask was then covered over by layers of adobe bricks and clay, and finally finished off with an enclosure of basalt columns.

fortune in her usual capriciousness decreed that this would come to light in the late afternoon (during the 1955 Drucker-Heizer expedition) just before the regular shift ended. "It was necessary to expose, record, photograph, and remove the find in the few hours of remaining daylight" because of fear of looting overnight. Offering No. 4 was hit upon under the floor of the Ceremonial Court. Sixteen figurines of jade or serpentine and six celts of the same materials had been arranged in a little group that obviously is meant to be a scene from real life. The figurines are typically Olmec, depicting men with loincloths and with bald or shaven heads that have been deformed in childhood by binding. One rather eroded figure stands with his back to a line of celts; the others are arranged about him and face him. Was he meant to be their leader? As the excavators, Drucker and Heizer, say, "We can only wonder."

But this is not the end of the story. After the offering had been originally placed and covered up, a series of floors of brightly colored clays—orange, rose, yellow, and white—was laid down over the entire court. Then, no one knows how many years later, somebody dug a pit down through these floors as far as the tops of the figurines and celts; and then, just as mysteriously, filled the pit up again. Why did they do this? Clearly, they had kept some sort of record of where this offering was and had seemingly been rechecking to make sure it was still there.

Burials have been mentioned. These might better be called "tombs," for they rival in richness some of the famous tombs of Old World archaeology. Most of them were uncovered by the Stirling expeditions of 1942 and 1943, for they belong to the final building phases of La Venta and thus lie near the surface. Unfortunately, the extremely acid soil of La Venta over the centuries has eaten away all traces of skeletons; nothing is left but the most imperishable of the loot buried with the dead Olmec lord. The three best-stocked sepulchers were in Mound A-2, on the north side of the Ceremonial Court and again, naturally, along the center line. The northernmost one is indeed curious, for it was built of gigantic basalt columns that in their natural form imitate tombs of wooden logs. On the limestone-slab floor were found the bundled remains of what had probably been two infants, surrounded (as in all La Venta burials) with brilliant red pigment. When these children, who must have been princes among their own people, were laid to rest, they were accompanied by a treasure-trove in jade: four figurines (one a seated woman with a tiny hematite mirror fragment on her breast), a jade clamshell, beads, ear ornaments, an awl-like object that probably was used to draw sacrificial blood, a jade sting-ray spine, and a pair of jade hands. Also in the same tomb were put a magnetite mirror and the tooth of an extinct giant shark.

Just to the south of this tomb was another, this time a sandstone sarcophagus. Again there was little or no trace of bones, but since it is big enough to contain an adult body and pigment covered its floor, it was surely a tomb. Its exterior was carved with a fearsome representation of a flame-browed werejaguar, while in its clay-filled cavity were found more beautiful

Archaeologist Eduardo Contreras of the 1955 La Venta expedition is seen tagging Offering No. 4, the most unusual Olmec treasure ever found. Buried about two feet below the surface, it consisted of tiny male Olmec figures made of jade, serpentine, and granite, each with a characteristic bald, deformed head, and all grouped for some ceremonial purpose beside jade and serpentine celts. OVERLEAF: *the same group displayed after it had been carefully removed, cleaned, and reassembled.*

jades: paper-thin ear spools (somewhat circular, outflaring objects set into the ear lobe), a serpentine figurine, and another "awl" for ceremonial bloodletting.

Then La Venta comes to an end. The cause and nature of its fate is lost in mystery, a mystery that we shall also see at the great Olmec center of San Lorenzo. All construction comes to a halt, no more tombs are built and stocked, no more offerings are made beneath its multicolored floors. Its rulers and people are gone, and year after year the nortes come howling in from the coast, shrouding the ruins of La Venta in drift sands. Olmec civilization had died.

Everything at La Venta is exotic, in the sense that it was brought from somewhere else. Even the brightly colored clays had been specially selected and brought to the island, for they are not indigenous. Likewise, the jade and serpentine (ton after ton of the latter) came from a distant and as yet unknown source. But the greatest wonder is that most of the volcanic basalt used in their monuments can only have come from the Tuxtla Mountains, sixty miles due west of La Venta.

Dr. Howel Williams is the leading expert on volcanoes. He has long been intrigued by the Olmec "problem"; and in 1960 he began explorations and studies with Robert Heizer that have largely solved the mystery of the rock source of the Olmec carvings at La Venta. By making thin sections of small pieces of rock taken from these monuments, it is possible to compare them under magnification with samples from identified lava flows in the Tuxtlas. It now seems that most of the La Venta carvings are made from basalt in the region of the Cerro Cintepec, an ancient cone among the many that make up the Tuxtla range. The lower slopes of these mountains are strewn with gigantic boulders of exactly the same kind of basalt. Apparently, the Olmec came here and either carved them on the spot or brought them to La Venta for working. Some are certainly large enough to make a fair-sized Colossal Head, and possibly their natural shape suggested the idea of the huge heads in the first place.

If this question has been answered, an even larger one remains. How did they ever get the stones to La Venta from the Tuxtlas? The engineering problems involved would be formidable even today. Certainly part of the journey could have been on enormous rafts, floated down the westernmost feeder streams of the Coatzacoalcos River, then along the coast, east to the mouth of the Tonalá. But they would have had to have been dragged at least twenty-five miles overland to reach navigable waters within the Coatzacoalcos drainage. Remember that the Colossal Heads, for instance, weigh an average of eighteen tons each. The problem was indeed formidable.

During the fourth and last building stage at La Venta, the rulers suddenly hit upon a new architectural device: they surrounded the Ceremonial Court with a kind of fence made up of huge columns of prismatic basalt. We have also seen the use of such columns in the large tomb to its north. Where did they get these? As one flies along the jungle-covered coastline of the Tuxtla region, prismatic basalt can be seen in

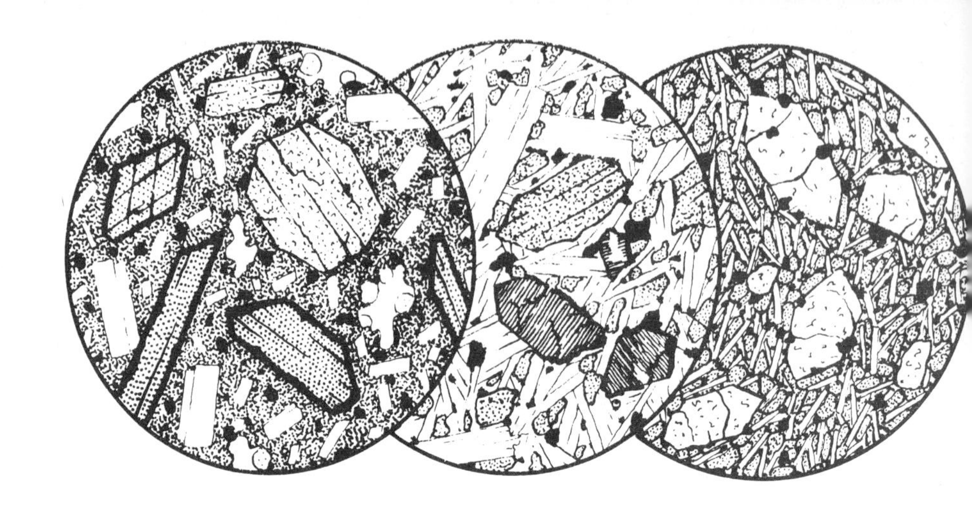

its natural state, the columns breaking off from the lava fields that once reached the sea. If this really was their source, the quarrying must have been a fearsome operation carried out from rafts, for this coast is often lashed by a heavy surf. One wonders how many great Olmec stones now rest on the bottom of the sea.

La Venta is dominated by its gigantic "pyramid," an earth or clay construction now measuring about one hundred feet in height. It sits upon a wide, low platform, on the south of which a number of fine monuments have been recovered. In all of the published plans of the main ceremonial complex of La Venta, the pyramid is shown looking as a pyramid should: four-sided, somewhat rectangular in a north-south direction, with a flat top. Back when the site was first mapped, an almost impenetrable jungle covered the structure, and the surveyor assumed, from a line of site cut across it, that it was perfectly normal in form. He was very, very wrong!

We may thank encroaching "civilization" for showing us the true picture, which is quite strange indeed. The oil camp of La Venta has now turned into a sizable and very ugly town; one of the most sordid red-light districts in Mexico lies at the very foot of the Great Pyramid, and the entire surface of this mighty construction has been completely cleared as a kind of park for the edification of the townsfolk and the ladies of easy virtue in the area.

Drucker and Heizer were the first to realize that this so-called pyramid was unlike anything they had ever seen before, and in 1968 Heizer and a University of California party made a detailed map of it. It now looks like a sort of truncated cone, but the sides of the cone are fluted; that is, ten enormous ridges, with gullies between, fan out on all sides. Some of this may be due to erosion, but the major part of this ridge-and-gully construction was deliberately made in ancient times. The whole thing resembles a gigantic, upside-down cupcake.

Heizer has tried to puzzle out the reason for such a construction. Actually, the closest parallel to the form of the Great Pyramid can be seen in the same Tuxtla Mountains from which the stone for the monuments came. Dozens of small volcanic cones dot the region around the beautiful Lake Catemaco, in the center of the Tuxtlas. Flying over this region one day, the thought suddenly struck him: the La Venta pyramid was an imitation volcano! Exactly the same sort of ridges and gullies can be seen fanning out from each cone. Here was an example of architecture imitating nature.

Why should the Olmec have done such a mad thing? Heizer has a final suggestion. We do not know where the Olmec homeland lay. Wherever it was, they already knew how to move and carve huge basalt boulders. The Tuxtla Mountains would be the logical place; so, on moving to La Venta, they took "a little bit of home" with them, to remind them of their volcano-surrounded origin point. A search for very ancient Olmec sites could and should be made in the Tuxtlas, but we may never find them. The same volcanoes were spewing cinders and lava until the eighteenth century, and the evidence may well lie buried a hundred feet deep, never to be uncovered.

In order to determine the source of the basalt from which the La Venta Olmec carved their monuments, geologist Howel Williams took tissue-paper-thin slices of stone and compared them to similar slices taken from lava flows in the Tuxtla Mountains (below), 60 miles to the west, and from a volcano some 80 miles to the southeast. Three La Venta samples (magnified at left) were so similar to the lava slices, it seems certain that these remote areas were the source of the stone.

5. SAN LORENZO

It is time now to talk of my own role in this story. I have been fascinated by the Olmec since I was a graduate student in anthropology, particularly after reading Covarrubias' exciting book, *Mexico South*. As I learned more about this controversial civilization, a conviction grew that Covarrubias, Caso, and Stirling had been right about it all along. For three subsequent field seasons I "labored in the vineyards," digging relatively simple Formative-stage sites on the Pacific Coast of Guatemala and in northwestern Costa Rica, until I was fairly certain about what pottery and other materials from this remote epoch should look like. Then in 1964 I decided to concentrate on San Lorenzo.

San Lorenzo is not one, but a group of three related archaeological sites. To reach the area, one travels to the grimy oil town of Minatitlán, situated on the Coatzacoalcos River about twenty-five miles above its mouth. Here one must search out and hire one of the dilapidated diesel boats (christened with such incongruous names as *Lusitania* and *Sacrificio*) that are the main form of transport on the river. The Coatzacoalcos and its tributaries drain all of the northern half of the Isthmus of Tehuantepec; at one point in its course, the river splits and flows about a large, swampy island called Tacamichapa, reputed by the local people to have belonged to Doña Marina, the famous Indian mistress of Cortés. The west branch, which skirts Tacamichapa, is the Chiquito River, and the boat enters it after two hours of travel. After another three to four hours' journey, passing between banks lined with fields of tall

Jungle-choked ravines such as this concealed many of San Lorenzo's major monuments.

Not until a topographical map of San Lorenzo had been completed was it realized that the ridges of the site were man-made. A simplified map shows a mirror symmetry to ridges on the south and west. No natural formations, the archaeologists reasoned, would appear so alike, and subsequent excavation confirmed their theory. The plateau stands about 150 feet high and is three-quarters of a mile long. What it may have represented to the Olmec is still not known.

corn alternating with patches of green jungle, the boat touches at its destination, the village of Tenochtitlán. This has been our home for three seasons of excavations (1966–1968). Walking up from the river edge through the village, one immediately notices that all of the native houses, built of poles or boards and thatched with palm fronds, are placed on artificial mounds, some of them quite high and long. Tenochtitlán is one of the three ancient sites in the area. It was so-named by a local schoolteacher, who, noting the size and number of ancient mounds there, decided that it must have been a great ancient city and so erroneously named it after the Aztec capital.

San Lorenzo is another of the archaeological sites in the area, located one and a half miles south-southwest of Tenochtitlán. The third is the little, palm-shaded village of Potrero Nuevo, one and three-quarter miles east-southeast of San Lorenzo. They are known collectively to archaeologists as San Lorenzo Tenochtitlán.

Again, it was Stirling who discovered the San Lorenzo Tenochtitlán group in 1945, having heard rumors in Coatzacoalcos that there had been found some very large carved stones upriver in that zone. By spring of the next year, Stirling, accompanied by his wife and Philip Drucker, had uncovered fifteen of the finest Olmec basalt monuments ever seen, including five of the largest and most beautiful Colossal Heads known to date. While the 1946 project was devoted to excavations at the most important site, San Lorenzo (where they made their camp), the collections had never been studied, and the mystery of the age of the Olmec monuments there remained unsolved.

I decided to get some money for a three-year project at San Lorenzo Tenochtitlán, but before I did so, I paid a visit to the area in December, 1964. In my innocence, I had not realized previously that I was walking into a hornet's nest! The last archaeologist to visit the zone, Alfonso Medellín Zenil, had almost been lynched there by the natives and left the village of Tenochtitlán under the protection of soldiers with submachine guns. Apparently the local populace had not taken kindly to the wholesale removal of their Olmec monuments to the Museum of Anthropology in Jalapa, Veracruz, without some form of compensation by the government, preferably in the form of a new school. The situation was still unresolved when I first went there. It has taken some very patient diplomacy over several years to convince the local populace of our good intentions. In the end, we succeeded, in large part because of the good will left by the Stirling group twenty years before.

Finally, word was received that the National Science Foundation in Washington, an independent fund-giving organization entirely supported by federal money, had decided to back my archaeological project over a period of three years. The first task was to build a camp, no simple job considering the spotty transportation along the river. For the first few months we lived in tents, while the rain came down day and night.

Next, of course, was to begin digging. Priority was devoted, in our first season, to discovering some sort of cultural sequence for the

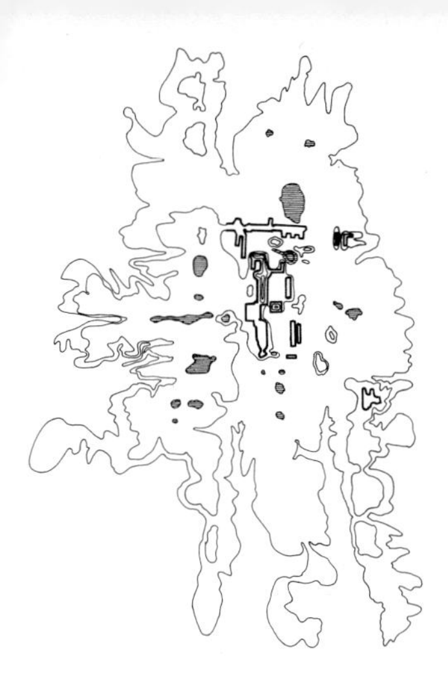

area. Here the principles of stratigraphy had to be applied and we were presented with a made-to-order situation along the riverbank just below the village of Tenochtitlán. The swirling waters that rush downstream during each rainy season had cut away remains of a clearly stratified series of villages; visible in the bank, beside numerous fragments of broken pottery, were charcoal-rich hearths, providing ample opportunity for radiocarbon determinations. At the same time, we set in excavating some recently discovered monuments at San Lorenzo. The major culture exposed at the riverbank and at San Lorenzo turned out to have pottery very similar to the Early Formative ceramics that I had been finding in my digging among village sites on the Pacific Coast of Guatemala, along with numerous Olmec figures. Most significantly, this culture, which we called San Lorenzo, proved to be definitely associated with the great Olmec monuments.

Naturally, I was anxious about the samples of charcoal from the 1966 season, which I had submitted to Dr. Minze Stuiver, the Dutch-born physicist who heads the Yale Radiocarbon Laboratory. When the results came in, they were indeed gratifying: the San Lorenzo culture, and therefore Olmec civilization in this area, dated to 1200–900 B.C.! This was older by several centuries than even La Venta.

Building a sequence of prehistoric cultures is usually a very complex business. After three seasons of stratigraphic work in the San Lorenzo zone, we can now reconstruct some sort of prehistoric picture in which the San Lorenzo phase appears just as one of a series of intermittent occupations. According to our present knowledge, the area was first settled back well beyond 1300 B.C. by pottery-using farmers who began altering the very strange San Lorenzo plateau. They were followed in turn by two other groups descended culturally from them. Then, after 1200 B.C., a band of outsiders with a vastly superior civilization took the place over; these were the Olmec of the San Lorenzo phase. They in turn declined around 900 B.C. and disappeared, and perhaps San Lorenzo Tenochtitlán was completely abandoned to the none-too-tender mercies of the jungle. And yet another group of persons come in the Middle Formative stage, this time possibly from La Venta itself, in what we are calling the Palangana phase. Here we have no C^{14} dates to help us, but this might have been between 600 and 300 B.C. Again, the area is deserted, until as late as 900 years *after* Christ, when a great wave of pioneering agriculturalists once again populates the entire district; some of these were undoubtedly living in the Coatzacoalcos drainage when the first Spaniards came through, and our workmen from Tenochtitlán may be their descendants.

The next task was to completely map San Lorenzo itself. Remember that it was at San Lorenzo that most of the great stones were discovered by Stirling. No previous map existed, and so the job had to be done. Ray Krotser, a retired civil engineer from California, was in charge of this project, and no easy job it turned out to be. The basic equipment was relatively simple: a plane table, on which the plastic film used for the map was

Virtually the only route to San Lorenzo is by aged river boats (below) from Minatitlán. The author's camp is seen in an air view, with the Chiquito River in the distance. Once the camp had been established, the site was cleared with machetes and fire to prepare it for mapping and excavation. At center, Ray Krotser, engineer of the project, is seen taking a "shot" with an alidade, the basic step in making a topographic map. Among the inconveniences

encountered were dense brush, clouds of mosquitoes, ticks by the millions, almost constant rain, and the deadly fer-de-lance (far right). The excavation area staked off, workers begin to dig, carefully peeling off each layer. As artifacts are uncovered, they are put in baskets according to stratigraphic level; then they are sent back to camp for washing and cataloguing. The excavation at lower right was made into a bank of what was perhaps a ball court.

North Court
Palangana
Central Court
South Court
Laguna 3
Laguna 4
Laguna 5
Laguna 6
Laguna 7
Laguna 8
Laguna 9
Laguna 10
Laguna 11
Laguna 12
Laguna 13
Laguna 19
Laguna 20
Laguna 21
Group D Ridge
Group C Ridge
Drain
Trough stones
Trough stones
N 1
N 2
N 3
M 5

The high point of the author's 1967 San Lorenzo expedition was the discovery of Monument 34, found on one of the two ridges running west from the site (the exact spot is noted on his map at left below). The figure, carved from basalt, was unlike any other ever found. The author (at left) scrapes dirt from the headless figure before it is taken from the ground. OVERLEAF: *Slung on poles, the half-ton monument is hauled back to camp by 17 workmen.*

affixed; an alidade, basically nothing more than a telescope mounted on a ruler and which sits on the plane table; and a stadia rod, a collapsible pole marked off in meters and centimeters. The rodman would place the stadia rod over a point, and it would be sighted by Krotser through his alidade. Parallel cross hairs within the telescope enclose a certain interval on the rod; this figure multiplied by one hundred produces the horizontal distance of the point over which the rod is held in meters. Other simple calculations provide the elevation of that point. Points of equal elevation are then connected by a contour line. This, in capsule, is how a contour map is made. But one has to take into consideration the heavy bush, the ticks (which were present by the millions), the mosquitoes, and, not least of all, deadly snakes like the fer-de-lance (we killed seven of these creatures during the 1967 season at San Lorenzo). Krotser discovered that only by sending large crews of machete wielders to cut down all the second-growth forest that covered large parts of San Lorenzo could all the mounds be mapped, right down to the smallest ones on which undoubtedly had sat the thatch-roofed dwellings of the ancients.

After many months' hard work, spread over two field trips, a map at a scale of 1:1000 was at last ready. It shows a very strange picture, indeed. We had known San Lorenzo as a plateau rising about 150 feet above the surrounding, savanna-covered plains; we had also known that it was deeply cut into by ravines on its north, west, and south sides, and that it was within or on the edge of these deep gullies that Stirling had found the Colossal Heads and other Olmec monuments for which the site is renowned. However, it was not until we had seen the final map—and also done quite a bit of deep digging at San Lorenzo—that we came to a previously unsuspected conclusion: that the ravines, the ridges that enclose them, and in fact the entire site as we now see it, represent a gigantic artifact, the result of human labor on a stupendous scale. Not only that, but the long, flat-topped ridges are obviously planned, for what purpose we cannot even guess. On the west, the Group C and Group D ridges, each about one hundred feet long, are mirror images of each other: every feature on one is matched by the identical feature on the other. The same thing is true of the pair formed by the much longer Southeast and Southwest ridges. Our deepest cuts in the San Lorenzo ridges reached culture-bearing layers down to twenty-five feet below ground level. There must be thousands upon thousands of tons of fill and debris in these finger-like constructions, all brought in basketloads on the backs of sweating Olmec.

The map also showed some other odd features of the site. There are over twenty depressions of various sizes and shapes dotting the surface of San Lorenzo. We have called these *lagunas*, as they contain water except at the height of the dry season, but if they were cleaned out they would probably provide water throughout the year. The lagunas are artificial, as can be seen not only from a trench we put into one of them (it had been lined with blocks of consolidated volcanic ash hauled up from the

Slightly larger than life-size, Monument 34 is probably of a ballplayer. Its uniqueness lies in the ratcheted-disk shoulder sockets, which indicate that the figure was once fitted with movable arms. Like nearly every other monument found at San Lorenzo, it had been mutilated (decapitated, in this instance); but as the author's work made clear, the whole destructive process was carefully carried out in accordance with a purposeful pattern.

deepest ravines), but also from the geometric shape that two of them have: they are six-sided. We have no real idea what their purpose was, but according to our present evidence the lagunas we now see were another product of Olmec civilization, that is, of its San Lorenzo phase.

San Lorenzo is about three-quarters of a mile long (north-south), and its surface is dotted with several hundred earthen mounds. The central group is clearly planned, with long, La Venta-like mounds enclosing courts. However, far more common are the undistinguished little bumps that archaeologists recognize as house mounds; from their distribution we know that houses were often arranged on two or three sides of tiny family plazas, like the extended-family dwellings of the Chinese farmer. If there are about two hundred of such house platforms, and five persons on an average dwelt within each house, then the resident population during the last years of the San Lorenzo phase might have been approximately one thousand. We dug into some of these house mounds and found broken metates for grinding corn still on the floor; those that we investigated on the Northwest ridge seem to have specialized in the manufacture of stone beads and ear ornaments, for a number of stone tools used to fashion these items were recovered.

Stirling has made some remarkably good guesses in his archaeological career. In only one of them has he been proved wrong: in his 1955 article on San Lorenzo Tenochtitlán, he surmised that most of the great carved stones which he had found on the edge of slopes or bottoms of the deep ravines at San Lorenzo had been pushed there by an invading people. Solving the mystery of what happened to the monuments, and why Stirling found them as he did, has provided us with some of our most exciting moments of discovery.

In our first season there, my assistant Richard Diehl, then a graduate student at Pennsylvania State University, was taken by local peasants to two stones projecting just above the ground, at different parts of San Lorenzo. Both being of basalt, Diehl immediately concluded that they were buried monuments and began digging. Both proved to be intimately associated with strata of San Lorenzo debris—potsherds, broken pottery figurines, and the like. Monument 21 (we number every monument in the order of its discovery) turned out to be a relief representation of a running animal, perhaps a dog or coyote. More important than its carving, however, was the fact that it had been placed face down over an offering of serpentine axes and blanks that had been used to make these tools. In other words, it had not been simply destroyed (it did show evidence of attempts at defacement as well), but had been carefully abandoned and buried with some show of ceremony. This offered us the possibility of finding other such buried monuments under the surface of San Lorenzo and associating them with our cultural sequence. The other stone, an enormous and brutally defaced altar (Monument 20), was similarly tied in with the San Lorenzo culture after careful excavations by Diehl and an archaeologist from the University of Veracruz, Francisco Beverido.

Another dramatic example of the Olmec's immense expenditure of effort, which, it would appear, was for no logical purpose, is this drainage system. Made of basalt, it consists of U-shaped stones capped with flat stones and packed in clay. More than 650 feet of the system has been found, representing some 30 tons of basalt that was hand-hewn with stone tools. The system's function was to drain a series of artificial ponds that probably had some religious meaning.

But the archaeological "payoff" came in March of 1967. We had known of an upright, stone stela sticking above the southern slope of our Group D ridge, on the western side of the site. In fact, Stirling writes of it in his field notes of 1946. A hunch led me to try excavating this undistinguished slab, Monument 23, to see if I could relate it to cultural layers and also, perhaps, to find offerings at its base. I never did find any offering, but this is of small moment compared to what was found. March 2 started out as gray and drizzly, typical of what we began to think of as "Olmec weather." I laid out a rectangular cut and had a laborer start digging, stripping off the deposits according to "natural" stratigraphy, that is, following differences in color, texture, and so forth.

The deposits proved to have very few sherds, and I began to wonder whether the ridge itself was not mainly sterile, a natural formation (we had yet to map this area); I was very much mistaken. Since there was very little room for Pedro Camaño, the workman whom I had set to this task, we laid out another square (Cut 2) to the north, in order to approach the stela from the side. This was the luckiest thing I have ever done, as my journal for March 8 records:

The main event of this day was the discovery of Mon. 34, a magnificent life-sized kneeling figure encountered in Cut 2. . . . It is just north of the stela, facing east. . . . There are no arms to the figure; rather, in their place are two ratcheted disks, perforated, which must have held movable stone arms—the largest jointed figure known! The right leg is tucked under the body.

It was time for a little reflection. Here was Monument 34, headless and therefore purposefully destroyed, but placed on a red gravel floor and covered up with a special fill containing a great deal of limestone and fragments of bentonitic rock brought up in basketloads from the deepest ravines, an event that we know took place late in the San Lorenzo phase. The stela had been set in the same floor and likewise covered up. My guess was that there would be more monuments similarly positioned, in a direct line heading north.

I turned out to be right. In the next month or so we hit upon, in this imaginary line, Monument 38, a fragment broken off some great altar; Monument 37, a crouching, headless figure of a gigantic jaguar that had been equipped with almost walrus-like tusks; Monument 40, a loose drain stone; Monument 41, an enormous, four-sided column with a brutal, low-relief figure of an Olmec deity; and the tiny Monument 43, perhaps the most diminutive Olmec "monument" ever found, representing a fantastic eight-legged creature, probably a spider. In place of eyes, it has the five-dot symbol known to be the Mesoamerican sign for jade.

Farther west on the same Group D ridge, I had been shown another stela similar to Monument 23, but much more broken. Careful excavations showed this also to be tied into the San Lorenzo phase deposits. One face was carved in a relief with a snarling, profile creature, somewhat resembling the old Olmec werejaguar, or Rain God, but which I think (on the evidence of the dragon-like body and the crossed bands in the eyes) to have been the great god known

as the Feathered Serpent. With our experience of the north-south line to the east, I began trenching away from this stela (Monument 30). Sure enough, more buried monuments began appearing in a line running west along the edge of the ridge. The last picked up was a magnificent sculpture of a caped personage holding in his hands the head of the deadly fer-de-lance, still so common in the area and probably an object of awe to the Olmec. Stylized wings appear in back of the snake's head, suggesting that this is another representation of the Feathered Serpent. Unfortunately, time had run out on the 1967 season; the thunder clouds of the approaching rains were already upon us. So to date we have not determined just how far west this particular line runs.

The whole series of monumental discoveries threw an entirely new light on San Lorenzo. We concluded from our work that the stones recovered by Stirling from the ravines had *not* been pushed there, but had fallen into them from the destructive forces of several millennia of erosion from the ridges above; that *all* of the San Lorenzo monuments had been carefully buried on a special floor on the top of the ridges or elsewhere on the site, then covered up with a specially selected fill; and that this had taken place near the end of the San Lorenzo phase. The natural question is: Who did it, and why? The fact that the same kinds of pottery and figurines typical of the San Lorenzo phase continue to be made for a while thereafter led us to think that some kind of internal Olmec revolt took place around 900 B.C. at San Lorenzo, as there is no evidence of an outside invasion.

The amount of pent-up hatred and fury represented by this enormous act of destruction must have been awesome, indeed. These monuments are very large, and basalt is a very hard stone. Wherever possible, heads were smashed from bodies, "altars" were smashed to pieces, and strange, dimpled depressions and slots were cut into Colossal Heads. There are no signs that wedges or the fire-and-water treatment were used to break up the larger stones; rather, I suspect that they built huge tripods over monuments, hoisted other monuments over these, and let them drop from great heights. Why was this done? Because the Olmec monuments must have stood for the class of leaders that held the tributary populace in such a firm grip, forcing from them incredible expenditures of labor. These stones must have been the symbols of all that had held them in thrall, and they destroyed these symbols with as much fervor as the Hungarian revolutionaries toppled the giant statue of Stalin in Budapest in 1956. But the Olmec must also have feared their power after the act, for by burying them with such care they removed the hated objects from their sight without incurring their posthumous wrath. Even Stalin's monuments did not have this honor.

The drain stone that was found in the north-south line of buried monuments is U-shaped in cross section and pecked out of a single piece of basalt. Other such stones were seen by Stirling lying in a ravine south of the Group C ridge, along with flat pieces of basalt. He suggested that the U-shaped stones had once been placed end-to-end and fitted with covers to

Twenty-one years after his first venture into San Lorenzo country, Matthew Stirling was on hand for the momentous discoveries of 1967, which more than substantiated his pioneering belief in the importance and vast age of the Olmec. Stirling is shown studying Monument 41, a huge basalt column on which is carved a barbaric-looking Rain God, with one hand clasping a withered arm. The column was found on a line with Monument 34, which was about 30 feet to the south.

make up a drain system, though he never did discover one so arranged. But most fortunately, we did, and its excavation consumed the better part of the 1968 season at San Lorenzo.

One day in April of 1967, my workman Agustin Camaño (the brother of Pedro Camaño and who under our training has become practically an archaeologist in his own right) mentioned that he had seen a section of a real drain system with stones just like those encountered by Stirling protruding from the slope of the same ravine, and that water gushed forth from it during the rainy season. I climbed with him down into the jungle-filled gully, and there it was, crying out for excavation! This was obviously a job for Ray Krotser, with his years of experience in civil engineering. While Paula, his wife, concentrated on trenching several pyramids elsewhere at the site, Krotser has, since completion of the map, been working full time on the drain. The trouble with our drain is that in places it is buried up to fifteen feet deep, hardly presenting an easy task to follow it out.

By April of the following year, Krotser was fairly sure he had found all of the system as it was, although part could have been destroyed in ancient times. The U-shaped stones had been placed end-to-end exactly as Stirling had guessed, within a shallow trench, and then covered over with the capstones. Finally the entire system was buried in fill. There is a principal drain line running west at a gentle degree of slope from the San Lorenzo plateau, and three subsidiary drain lines that tie into it from the south at a steep angle. The sophistication of the joints between the branch and main lines prove the Olmec to have been accomplished engineers.

The size of the operation is particularly impressive (nothing that the Olmec did was on a small scale, or easy). The main line as we excavated it is 558 feet long, with 98 feet of subsidiary lines! There are no less than thirty tons of basalt in the system, all brought in from the outside, and all worked with great precision and without the benefit of metal tools. What was the system made for? We wish we knew. Several of the U-shaped stones at the head of the main line are perforated, as though these were the entrances for the water. If this was the start of the system, then what had it been draining? Mention has been made of the ponds or lagunas on the surface of San Lorenzo. We know from the geometric shape of some of these and from a cut made into one laguna that they are man-made. Several lie to the north and south of the drain head; Ray Krotser calculates that these lagunas could once have been part of a super-laguna, the approximate center of which would have been above this point. This still does not tell us why they would have built the lagunas, and less why one of them should be drained with such an elaborate and time-consuming system. One thinks of the sacred pools of the temples and palaces of India and Ceylon, to which priests and the faithful repair for holy ablutions during festivals. Quite possibly we are confronted with the same thing among the Olmec of three thousand years ago. At any rate, whether ritual or not, we have here the first system of water control yet known for the New World.

Among the most important new pieces of equipment put to use at San Lorenzo was the cesium magnetometer, which in a few hours detected four buried monuments that otherwise might never have been found. The instrument's batteries strapped to his belt, a scientist (near right) works over an area not far from the drainage system. One of the prize stones located, Monument 52 (far right), is yet another representation of the Rain God, in purest Olmec style.

Every archaeologist has sometimes wished he had some instrument in his hands that could see what lies underground and direct him to the best places to dig. Since World War II, the physical scientists have come very close to realizing this dream. Among the instruments that have been developed in the United States and abroad are the resistivity meter, which detects objects or constructions by passing an electric current through the soil; seismic instruments, which perform roughly the same task by means of shock waves; and periscopes, which can be lowered through holes drilled through the roof of underground tombs. None of these, however, has quite fulfilled the promise that they seemed to hold out to archaeology: there are just too many "bugs" in these and other systems. Ground water, for instance, can seriously affect the readings of a resistivity meter.

In a different class altogether has been an instrument called a magnetometer. This was developed to detect differences in the intensity of the magnetic field over any part of the earth at a given moment. Such variations are called anomalies, and they are sometimes caused by buried objects containing a fairly large amount of iron. Magnetometers have been used to detect mineral and oil deposits, locate avalanche victims in the Alps, and have even been successfully used in the search for the lost submarine *Thresher*. In 1964 Varian Associates of Palo Alto, California, leaders in the magnetometry field, began work in locating the ancient Greek city of Sybaris, deeply buried under layers of silt since medieval times, but known to have existed as a flourishing (and sybaritic) settlement in southern Italy. Working in cooperation with Dr. Froelich Rainey of the University Museum (University of Pennsylvania), long an advocate of the use of physical detection methods in archaeology, the magnetometry specialists located walls and buildings of what may have been the famous city. Only future excavation—very difficult because of the high water table—will show whether this is really Sybaris.

In the 1968 season, I was contacted by Dr. Rainey and the Varian people. They wanted to try out an extremely sensitive model, the cesium magnetometer, on San Lorenzo; here, the high magnetic intensity of the iron-rich basalt monuments and the low background "noise" of the surrounding deposits should pay off spectacularly. It sounded too good to be true, but we decided to give it a try. The Varian team, headed by Sheldon Breiner, arrived on March 27, bringing with them an instrument that looked like a tin can mounted on a rod. The "tin can" contained cesium gas, which produces a radio frequency signal proportional to the intensity of the anomaly passed over; it is so sensitive that it can measure variations of one part in five million of the earth's magnetic field. The signal is picked up by a small receiver worn (along with forty pounds of batteries) on the belt, and transformed into clicks and into numbers.

The next day, Breiner and his assistants began walking over a part of San Lorenzo, watched by curious but skeptical archaeologists and workmen. All at once the magnetometer began clicking furiously. "Dig here," said Breiner.

Eventually, the workman's pick grazed over a monument, buried at exactly the depth predicted by Breiner. Not far away, the instrument began to record another anomaly, and again a monument was excavated in that spot. Within a week's time we had had the opportunity to dig in four of the places shown as magnetic anomalies, and all proved to be broken basalt monuments. Three were but fragments broken from much larger stones, but one (Monument 52) turned out to be one of the most beautiful and complete Olmec statues ever found at San Lorenzo: a standing werejaguar with snarling mouth and cleft head, the great Olmec Rain God himself—a fitting close to our archaeological work at San Lorenzo. The astonishment of the non-physicists standing around to watch was complete.

The future possibilities of the cesium magnetometer are truly awesome. In a survey made over a fraction of the site, Breiner and his assistants were able to place on our map about thirty-five other anomalies that surely are going to turn out to be monuments. There must be many hundreds remaining to be excavated, buried in that remote act of destruction, soon to come to light for the benefit of Mexico's museums and the Mexican people. Our only regret is that we did not have this "magic wand" with us from the very beginning of the project.

We have answered many questions at San Lorenzo over three seasons; but, as with any thorough archaeological project, we have left several unanswered and have raised others that had not even been predicted. For example, the rulers of the area, the men who created the great Olmec civilization of the San Lorenzo phase, came from elsewhere—but we have no idea where. At the time of their arrival the place was already inhabited, and it may well be that three of the crudest relief sculptures that we have found were the work of pre-San Lorenzo people (such as Monument 41). This elite class surely must have come from a region where they already knew how to work and transport great basalt boulders. The perfection of their carving suggests a long prior period of artistic development. I have suggested a homeland in the Tuxtla Mountains, but we must not take this as more than a suggestion.

I also feel that high culture came to an end at San Lorenzo through a violent internal revolt. After 900 B.C., when San Lorenzo began returning to the jungle, the torch of Olmec civilization must have been passed to La Venta, the island capital in the Tonalá swamps fifty-five miles away.

The most important questions that can be asked are these, however: What were the factors that allowed San Lorenzo to be the first civilized center of Mesoamerica and probably of the New World? How did they manage to maintain this high level for three centuries? What were their population, their social and political structure, and their economy? And why might revolution have finished them off? There are no written documents for this epoch, as distant from us as the Trojan War, so we can never be exactly sure of what went on. But there are other ways to the truth, which we will examine shortly.

6. EXPANSION OF THE OLMEC

Among Mexico's thousands of archaeological sites, one of the most exciting is Chalcatzingo, only a few hours to the southeast of Mexico City, near the eastern border of the little state of Morelos. One drives over the pine-covered mountains surrounding the capital, then drops down into a region that is almost semitropical by comparison with the 7,500-foot-high Valley of Mexico. Much of Morelos is irrigated, with mile after mile of bright green sugar-cane fields. Passing the town of Cuautla, a strange sight meets the eye: three great rock hills rising above the plain, with sheer walls of basalt to which only an occasional wild fig tree can cling. Like Shiprock, the gigantic butte in our own southwestern desert, these hills apparently represent the cores of volcanoes long since eroded away.

It is the central peak, so reminiscent of some sacred mountain among the Australian aborigines, that concerns us here. A mighty cliff terminates in a steep talus slope, strewn with gigantic boulders that must have tumbled down many thousands of years ago. A long, hot climb to the top of the talus brings you to one of the great monuments of the Olmec civilization. Petroglyph 1 of Chalcatzingo is a nine-foot high relief scene pecked into the flat surface of one of these boulders. It depicts a richly attired personage seated on a throne, and carrying in its arms a long object reminiscent of the so-called "ceremonial bars" of the Classic Maya. Surprisingly, this figure is female, with wrap-around skirt, long hair, and towering headdress. She is seated within what at first seems to be a cave, but which on closer inspec-

This hollow figurine of a baby in Olmec style is from a cemetery at Las Bocas.

tion turns out to be a monstrous mouth of a creature, the eye of which appears at top. Sprouting corn plants are placed at the corners of the "mouth," while at the top of the scene are three stylized cumulus clouds from which rain pours. Rain drops can be seen elsewhere on the relief, and also in the headdress and on the skirt of the woman. To her right, from the mouth-cave, scroll-like figures undulate: Are they smoke plumes from burning copal incense?

Now, this relief is in the purest Olmec style, directly comparable to that on Stela 3 at La Venta. It was first described as long ago as 1934 by the Mexican historian Eulalia Guzman. Further petroglyphs at Chalcatzingo were also seen by her, and more have been discovered in recent years by Dr. Carlo Gay, a retired Italian industrialist who has made the study of the ancient Olmec his vocation. Petroglyph 2 is not far north of the "lady in the cave." This scene, while also typically Olmec, is quite different, and it emphasizes a theme that can be seen elsewhere in Olmec sites beyond the "heartland": conquest. On the right is a goateed man sprawled back upon a little werejaguar idol. His bound wrists and nudity show him to be a captive, humiliated in typical Mesoamerican style by having his genitals bared. To his left, two Olmec warriors, wearing werejaguar masks and carrying paddle-shaped clubs, menace him, while another figure walks off stage with a club that seems to be turning into a corn plant.

A similar scene of violence, perhaps more symbolic, is Petroglyph 4, with two rampant Olmec jaguars attacking prone men (one of whom wears what is probably a concave mirror on his chest). The present position of the rock on which it is carved suggests that this, and several other reliefs at the site, are not in their original position, but have slipped or rolled down from above, perhaps during the earthquakes that are not uncommon in Morelos. But most significant of all is Petroglyph 5, which has been unfortunately damaged in the last few years by thoughtless people taking plastic molds for reproduction. A strange serpent with fanged mouth is devouring another prone human, its undulating body surrounded by scroll-like "lazy S" signs; a short wing is tucked on the back part of the profile head. What could this creature be? We shall defer the full answer until the next chapter. But suffice it to say here that this is one of the strongest pieces of evidence for the worship of the great god Quetzalcóatl, the Feathered Serpent, by the Olmec.

What were the Olmec doing at Chalcatzingo, some two hundred miles due west of the Olmec heartland, among rivers that flow down to the Pacific? The problem of the significance of Chalcatzingo is part of the larger problem of the Olmec expansion over much of central Mexico, down to Guerrero near the Pacific Coast, and thence southeast to the Pacific slopes of the Central American countries, as far as El Salvador. The circumstance of finding hundreds of beautiful Olmec objects in Morelos and Guerrero has led several archaeologists to propose either of these two states as the Olmec homeland, instead of Veracruz and Tabasco. Miguel Covarrubias, in particular, was an advocate of Guerrero. I think that this proposition is highly unlikely, and that another expla-

In the highlands south of Mexico City, at the base of a volcanic cliff, is the relief carving at left, known as Petroglyph 1, from Chalcatzingo. It shows (below) a woman in elaborate headdress seated within a mouth-like cave, from the entrance of which spew forth spirals representing smoke or incense, while life-giving rain falls from three clouds overhead. An exceptional work of art, the carving also offers solid evidence of Olmec control over Mexico's central highlands.

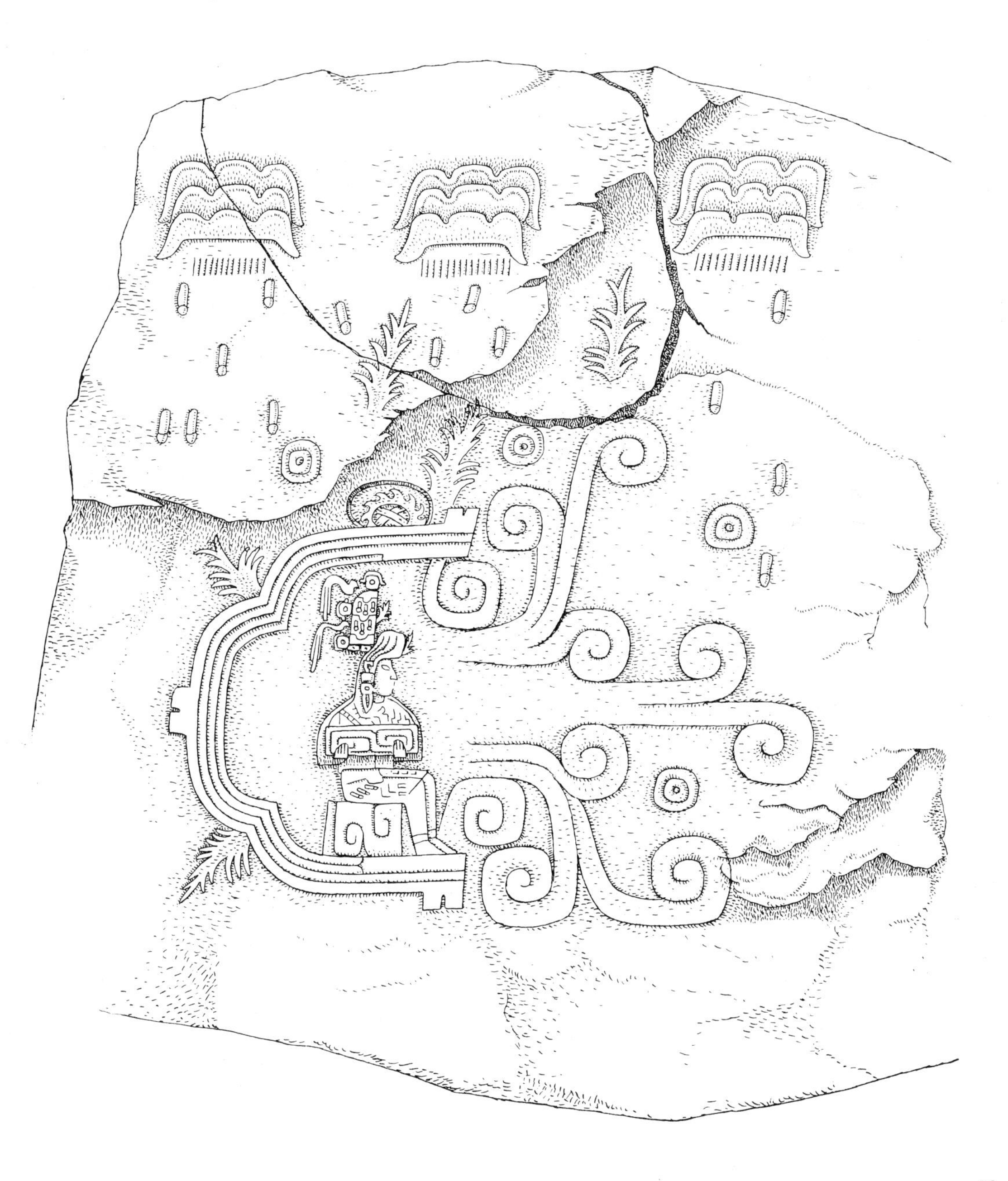

The genius of the Olmec is found not only in their colossal basalt monuments and stone reliefs, but in hundreds of tiny clay figurines. These are from graves at Las Bocas, 35 miles east of Chalcatzingo. Most of the figures retrieved have been white with red pigment rubbed into them, and they usually represent people in far more informal and animated poses than do the larger Olmec works. What special symbolism they may have had, if any, remains a mystery.

nation is possible for the Olmec presence here.

Basically, my position is that the Olmec erupted into southwestern Mexico, and in particular into the drainage of the great Balsas River, because there was something that they needed in the heartland which was not present along the Gulf Coast. This "something" was undoubtedly jade, the very symbol of Olmec wealth and authority. As mentioned earlier, Classic Maya jade is known to have come from the Motagua River valley in Guatemala, but nobody knows for sure the source of the fine, blue-green jade so prized by the Olmec. The metamorphic formations in which jade develops are unknown in the heartland. The case of Guerrero is different. One of the disagreeable by-products of the present demand among collectors for Olmec art has been the large-scale production of high-quality fakes for this market. For many years now, the picturesque town of Taxco in Guerrero has been the center of this industry. These fakes are fashioned from exactly the same kind of jade as was used by the Olmec themselves. Fakers are a close-mouthed lot, and, as might be imagined, they are not anxious to let their jade source be known. But according to local rumor, it comes from the hills near Arcelia, seventy-five miles west of Taxco and right on the Balsas River, in a geologically metamorphic region.

Another prized substance in great demand among the Olmec of San Lorenzo and La Venta was serpentine. Since jade is found in serpentine strata, this could also have come from Guerrero, but a more likely source lies somewhat closer at hand, namely, in the state of Puebla, between Veracruz and the Valley of Mexico. What I am suggesting is a jade-serpentine route among the Olmec of three thousand years ago, leading up from the Gulf Coast and through Puebla into the volcanic highlands of central Mexico, then down the other side through Morelos into the Balsas drainage of Morelos, all under the control of Olmec groups that were at the same time (as among the far later Aztec) both warriors and merchants.

Evidence in support of this idea has recently come from an archaeological survey of Morelos made in 1966–1967 by Dr. David Grove of the State University of New York. Grove has found that all of those Morelos sites which have produced Olmec material lie at strategic points along major passes or connecting valleys, usually at the foot of cliffs that would have afforded some means of defense. Chalcatzingo itself stands near the entrance to one of the few passes—actually a long plain—running through the hills separating Morelos from western Puebla. Crossing this pass to the east, one enters the cane-covered valley of Izúcar de Matamoros, in Puebla. At its eastern side is the now-famous archaeological site of Las Bocas.

Grove has remarked that Las Bocas in appearance strikes the observer as a miniature Chalcatzingo, with its location at the foot of a Chalcatzingo-like hill and cliff. No other ancient habitation in Mexico has produced such beautiful ceramics as Las Bocas. Unfortunately, all of what we know about Las Bocas comes from offerings looted from what must have been some of the richest burials ever found in Mesoamerica. In private collections in Mexico

and the United States are lovely pottery bowls with grooved designs showing the Olmec motif of the jaguar paw that is at the same time a wing; these bowls are absolutely identical to those made by the San Lorenzo Olmec. In these same graves have been found pottery vessels shaped as fantastic animals—birds, monkeys, fish, and so forth; clay rollers that were most likely used to impress various designs in red pigment on the skins of young ladies; and magnificent little white-ware pottery figurines of Olmec individuals, both men and women, some luxuriously reclining on elbows or pillows. But Las Bocas is best known for its extraordinary, oversize, hollow pottery figures. These depict infantile creatures that are probably human, but whose Mongoloid features, sexlessness, and occasional obesity suggest some glandular disorder. They are, in fact, almost duplicates of the little humanoid, werejaguar children shown on the Quintuplet Altar at La Venta, and may be related to the great Rain God himself.

The near-identity of the Las Bocas offerings with what we know to be the perfectly ordinary dinnerware and household toys of San Lorenzo raises the possibility that Las Bocas represents a military-commercial outpost of Veracruz in the twelfth to tenth centuries B.C. (An analogy might be the fortified settlements south of Hadrian's Wall in Britain, on the very edge of the Roman Empire, in which items of everyday use in the imperial capital attained an extra prestige in these distant military posts.)

Such "colonial" Olmec sites are found in the Valley of Mexico itself. Recent C^{14} dates show that these sites are older than any other Formative settlements yet known for this important highland basin. Tlapacoya is one of these, an Olmec village or small town once located on the shores of a volcanic island now linked to the mainland through drying-up in post-conquest times of the great lake that filled the basin. There, Dr. Paul Tolstoy has demonstrated that an Olmec occupation underlies what was long thought to have been the earliest ceramic culture of the valley; in the Yale Radiocarbon Laboratory we have dated this to 1070–940 B.C.

Tlatilco is, with Tlapacoya, the greatest Formative site of the Valley of Mexico. Tlapacoya, following the trade-route hypothesis, lies at the Valley of Mexico end of the major pass leading south into eastern Morelos and western Puebla; the present-day road from Mexico City over to the Valley of Toluca on the west (where Olmec ceramics are also known) happens to run right through what is left of the site of Tlatilco. I say "what is left" because there is now little more to be seen there than a series of huge, gaping pits left by the excavation of clay for the brickyards that have been exploited in this zone for many years. Tlatilco was, in fact, discovered by brickyard workers, who began (in the early 1940's) to uncover burials in their search for clay. Objects from these burials came to the attention of local collectors, in particular, Miguel Covarrubias, who quickly realized that here was a find of the greatest importance: a site with demonstrably pre-Classic pottery and figurines, associated with objects that were surely Olmec. Thus, Covarrubias became convinced that the Olmec civilization of the Gulf Coast was extremely ancient.

The major settled area in the Valley of Mexico during the time of the Olmec was Tlatilco. Here, over many generations, people buried their dead beneath their homes, one grave often intruding on another from an earlier time. The graves contain remarkable pottery, such as the parrot-bottle at left, and a jumble of human remains that may include actual Olmec bones. Whatever their origin, these people lived under Olmec influence.

Tlatilco has been called a cemetery, but the concept of a separate burial ground is alien to the Mesoamerican mind, and only came to Mexico with the Christian missionaries. The typical way of interring a deceased family member was by placing him in a grave, along with objects that were important to him in his life and accompanied by offerings of food and drink, below the very floor of his own house—preferably directly beneath his *petate*, or sleeping mat. Even today, among the isolated Maya of the Chiapas highlands in southeast Mexico, while a person receives burial in a Christian cemetery, the relatives will scoop up some dirt below his petate and scatter it over the grave. Many hundreds, perhaps even thousands, of graves have been found at Tlatilco. The fact that many of these have disturbed others placed earlier shows that they were subfloor burials and not marked graves.

It is an archaeological tragedy that there has never been a serious study of the thousands of pottery vessels, clay figurines, stone tools, and other artifacts found by archaeologists in Tlatilco. If there had been, Tlatilco would surely turn out to have had a long and complex sequence of occupation. One thing is now certain, though: the graves with definitely Olmec material are the earliest, being radiocarbon-dated to the twelfth century B.C. and therefore coeval with the height of San Lorenzo. These are obviously the remains of the same people who were at Las Bocas in Puebla and probably also at Chalcatzingo: Olmec warrior-traders. Under their stimulus, Tlatilco grew into a small town, along a small river flowing into the great

Among the most fascinating pieces found in the graves at Tlatilco are tiny clay figurines depicting ordinary people—magicians, dancers, women with babies, ballplayers, children—done in a style quite different from that of the Olmec, and displaying a humor not seen in Olmec art. Amazing numbers of these figures were modeled, like gingerbread men, in a manner that was indigenous to the area and that was carried on long after the period of Olmec power had been superseded.

lake. Located among soils fertile for corn agriculture, the local population could also call upon the rich food resources of the lake itself—especially waterfowl—while hunting deer and other four-footed game in the hills above the town. Eventually, most likely after the decline of great Olmec sites such as San Lorenzo on the Gulf Coast, Olmec influence wanes at Tlatilco. There is instead a recrudescence of a native, peasant culture that had been there all the time. Civilization was not to touch central Mexico again until the last few centuries before the Christian Era, when the Teotihuacán culture was taking form.

This local peasant element coexisted with the Olmec at the site. In a typical burial of the era, the skeleton (showing the weird, front-and-aft cranial deformation favored by the Olmec) is extended full length, face up; all around it and mingled with the bones might be dozens of offerings, usually including at least one San Lorenzo-style bowl. But other vessels (which presumably contained food to sustain the deceased in the other world) are clearly of native manufacture, especially graceful, long-necked clay bottles with gourd-like bodies. Singly or in clusters also appear the little, solid, handmade figurines for which Tlatilco is noted. These are of the utmost delicacy, usually showing tiny slant-eyed ladies with grass skirts or bereft of any clothing. The most lovely of all depict charming females with grossly exaggerated thighs and rumps. In fact, these early Tlatilco figurines exhibit the widest range of activities: ballplayers, magicians, acrobats, dancers, mothers holding their babies in cradle boards, couples seated on couches. Curiously, both the ballplayers and dancers often wear small masks fitting over the lower part of the face; such miniature masks of clay have been encountered in the graves.

Covarrubias had a theory about the development of civilization in the Valley of Mexico, which ran something like this: a group of Olmec aristocrats took over what had previously been a classless peasant society. The social and political contradictions between these two eventually led to a class state, which ultimately turned into Teotihuacán. This idea, so obviously stemming from Marxist political theory, is now somewhat outdated, since we are sure that the Olmec civilization was so ancient that it could have had little to do directly with the rise of Teotihuacán. Nonetheless, I think it likely that the number of Olmec at Tlatilco may have been small, and they may have functioned as a nobility and have had to adapt somewhat to the local culture.

It can be argued that there may never have actually been any Gulf Coast Olmec at all at Tlatilco and Tlapacoya: that the Olmec objects there were portable trade items sent up from the heartland. But this cannot be true of Chalcatzingo, where there are monumental Olmec rock carvings, nor can it hold for the painted caverns of Juxtlahuaca, tucked away in the hills of Guerrero.

How many tourists, speeding down the highway from Mexico City to the beaches of Acapulco, know that they are passing within a few dozen miles of the oldest paintings in the New World? What the casual tourist does see, how-

ever, are bone-dry, cactus-and-mesquite covered hills, as desiccated as anything in the Tehuacán Valley. Most of central and northern Guerrero is this way. The only relief from the dusty landscape is provided by the river valleys, many of which drain into the Balsas River on their way to the Pacific Ocean. It is these valleys which provide the only really productive agriculture possible for the area, and that only because they are irrigated. No right-thinking Olmec would ever have settled here without the knowledge of irrigation techniques; minus this knowledge, the only farming possible in central Guerrero would have been on the level of MacNeish's primitive, preceramic Tehuacán Indians.

If our tourist, after passing over the Acapulco highway through the oven-hot Cañon del Zopilote (Canyon of the Vulture), continues a little beyond the Guerrero capital, Chilpancingo, he will note a dirt road leading off to the east. This road takes one through a beautiful but narrow irrigated valley, filled with fields of green corn and sugar cane; this valley is part of the watershed of the Río Papagayo (Macaw River), which meets the Pacific Coast just east of Acapulco. Juxtlahuaca Cave lies at the eastern end of the valley, its principal entrance on the side of a hill overlooking the wild mountains of southeastern Guerrero. Juxtlahuaca has been known since the 1930's, but the immense significance of its paintings was only realized in July, 1966, when Carlo Gay, accompanied by Gillett Griffin of Princeton University, explored the cave and concluded that these paintings were, in fact, completely Olmec. Their publication attracted world-wide attention (and some jealousy among many, supposedly "professional," archaeologists).

The descent to the paintings through the caverns (which I visited in April, 1968) is reminiscent of Jules Verne's *Journey to the Center of the Earth.* The guide, Andrés Ortega, is equipped with kerosene lanterns, but knows the cave so well he could probably find his way out in the dark. Passing chambers filled with bats (the floors and walls of these are sometimes covered with scurrying, giant cockroaches), the descent begins through narrow passages and occasionally enormous chambers, resplendent with huge stalactites and curtain-like formations. The Hall of the Dead, which must be passed on the way to the paintings, is one of these chambers, a vast room in which a massive cave-in has piled the floor high with fallen rock. Among these rocks, and in some cases under them, are human skeletons, some extended like the Tlatilco burials, but others in a crouching, fetal posture. All are covered with stalagmitic crust. Dr. Gay has counted the remains of three children and eight adults, but others have subsequently been found by Andrés Ortega; in one place, a tiny chamber surrounded by stalactites contains a single skull, staring out into darkness with hollow eyes.

Thirty-one hundred feet in from the entrance one encounters a strange, artificial canal (or drain) dug into the slippery, red clay floor of the cave. This canal zigzags 250 feet into the Gallery of the Drawings and the Hall of the Serpent, low chambers that must have represented to the Olmec the very end of the cav-

Within a cave at Juxtlahuaca, nearly a mile from the entrance, is a wall painting some 3,000 years old that may well be the oldest in the New World. Although its existence has been known for some time, it has only recently been recognized as Olmec. On the right a black-bearded king wearing a feathered headdress, striped tunic, gauntlets and leggings of jaguar skin brandishes an unidentifiable object before a kneeling person who is possibly a captive.

erns, the absolutely most inaccessible place (thirty years ago, Ortega's brothers opened a tunnel at the back through which one may crawl into an underground paradise, a series of lake-filled chambers with crystalline walls, the counterpart of that inner sea encountered by the heroes of the Verne novel).

The paintings are four thousand feet in from the entrance, over three-quarters of a mile. The artist or artists who executed them must have done so by the light of pine torches. In the Gallery of the Drawings is the most majestic scene: a great Olmec personage with jet-black beard is attired with a head ornament of green quetzal plumes, tunic painted with wavy bands of red, yellow, and black, and probably a brown cape thrown over one shoulder. He wears gauntlets made from the paws and hide of a jaguar, while his legs are garbed in jaguar skin as well. In his right hand he carries a strange object that is directed toward another human figure crouching at his feet; this individual has a small goatee and a face painted black, while his body is painted red. The entire composition is a masterpiece of Olmec art and the only polychrome representation known for the entire Olmec repertory. The final chamber, the Hall of the Serpent, is so-called from the great snake painted in bright red on a slab jutting out from the wall of the cave. In its eye is the familiar "crossed-bands" motif of the Olmec, and above the brow are short, green plumes: here again is our Feathered Serpent. Facing the serpent is another painting, this of a feline creature apparently jumping at the snake. Its head and body are colored red, but over the back is a spotted skin: Is this a mountain lion wearing the disguise of a jaguar?

What does all this signify? In the first place, the principal scene is probably secular, representing a great Olmec ruler. His jaguar-paw gloves are exactly what are worn by great civil leaders among the Classic Maya of fifteen hundred years later as symbols of kingship—even today among the conservative highland Maya, hereditary chiefs are believed to have a spiritual relationship with the jaguar. The Feathered Serpent is a religious theme, but in late Post-Classic Mexico the rulers were considered to be descendants of that god. Among the Mesoamericans, as with all peoples, it is very hard to keep secular and profane separate. There must have been an extraordinary mystery to this subterranean shrine. If one could only conjure up the scene of its dedication—a great procession of Olmec royalty, lit by the flare of pine torches, and probably accompanied by chanting and drumming. But time has removed all but these extraordinary paintings, which remain to fascinate us with their strange power.

That the Olmec were in Guerrero cannot now be doubted; that they were after Guerrero jade is a strong possibility; and that they could have only settled here after irrigation had been developed in the highlands (perhaps around 1000 B.C.) is a certainty. These pioneers must have felt themselves in a very strange environment, so different from the wet forests of the southern Gulf Coast. But they were not content to colonize only Guerrero and central Mexico. Scattered Olmec monuments are found much farther to the southeast, along the hot,

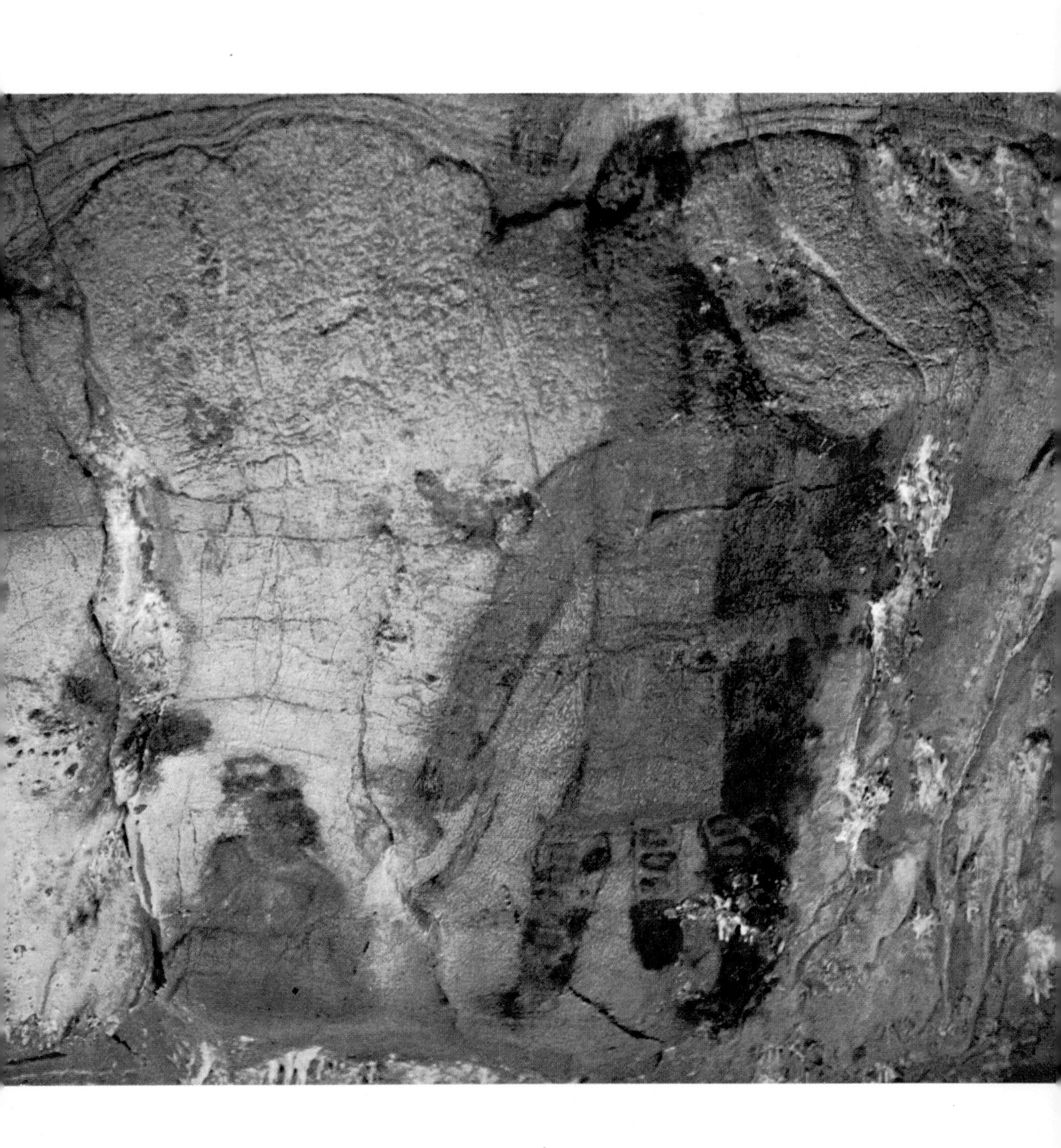

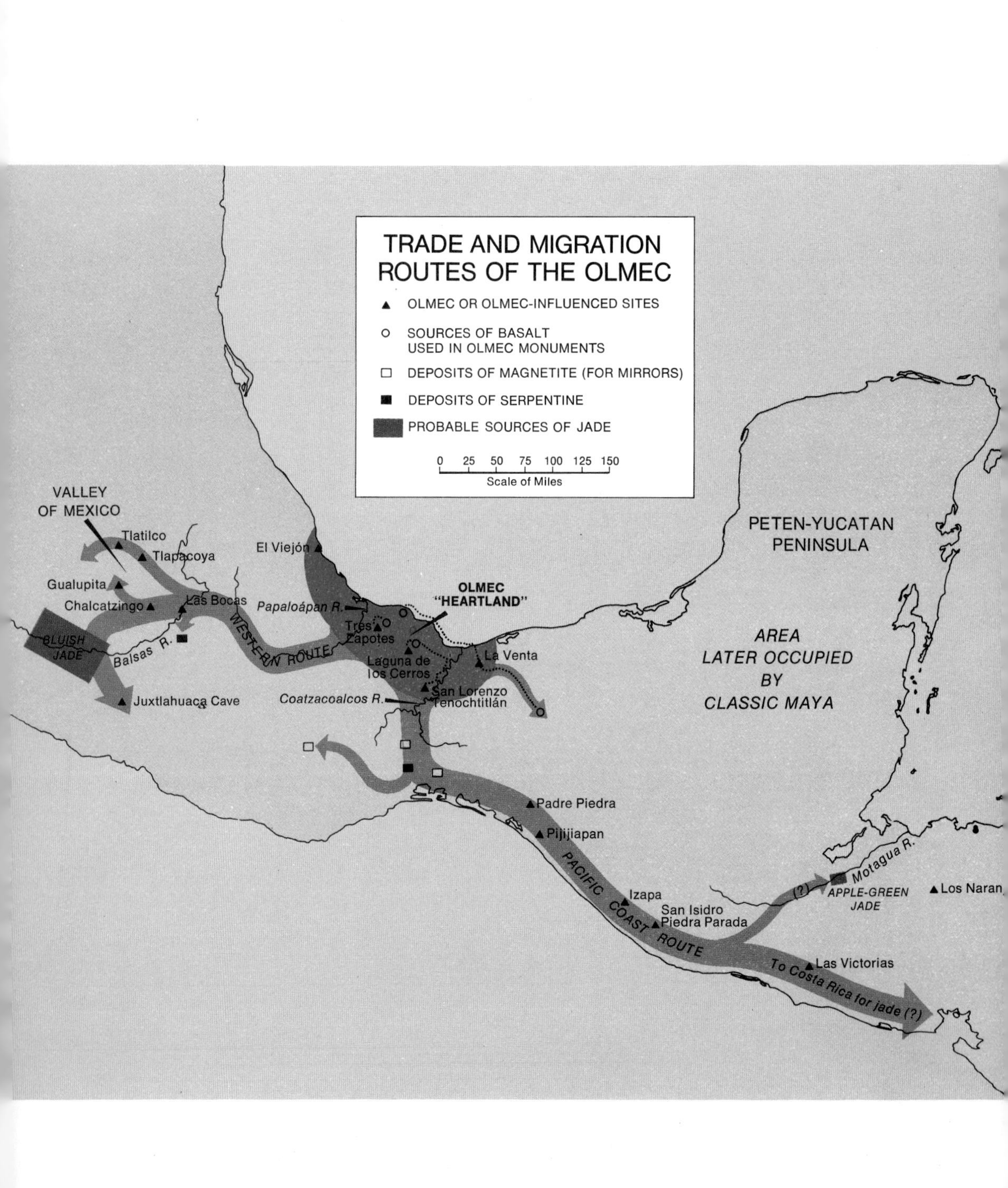

TRADE AND MIGRATION ROUTES OF THE OLMEC
OLMEC OR OLMEC-INFLUENCED SITES
SOURCES OF BASALT USED IN OLMEC MONUMENTS
DEPOSITS OF MAGNETITE (FOR MIRRORS)
DEPOSITS OF SERPENTINE
PROBABLE SOURCES OF JADE
0 25 50 75 100 125 150
Scale of Miles
VALLEY OF MEXICO
Tlatilco
Tlapacoya
Gualupita
Chalcatzingo
Las Bocas
BLUISH JADE
Balsas R.
WESTERN ROUTE
Juxtlahuaca Cave
El Viejón
Papaloápan R.
Tres Zapotes
OLMEC "HEARTLAND"
Laguna de los Cerros
La Venta
San Lorenzo Tenochtitlán
Coatzacoalcos R.
PETEN-YUCATAN PENINSULA
AREA LATER OCCUPIED BY CLASSIC MAYA
Padre Piedra
Pijijiapan
PACIFIC COAST ROUTE
Izapa
San Isidro Piedra Parada
Motagua R.
(?)
APPLE-GREEN JADE
Los Naran
Las Victorias
To Costa Rica for jade (?)

The expansion of the Olmec over many centuries was chiefly motivated by their trading for luxury materials—mostly jade for ceremonial purposes—that were unobtainable in their own heartland. The map depicts the main thrusts of Olmec migration, which, some archaeologists now believe, may have reached as far south as Costa Rica (not shown). It appears that they built no roads, but followed rivers and kept to the natural routes and mountain passes.

fertile plain that reaches from the Pacific side of the Isthmus of Tehuantepec down through Guatemala and into El Salvador. Most of these are fairly simple reliefs pecked onto the surface of natural boulders, no match for the wonderful carvings of the heartland, or for Chalcatzingo, for that matter. The end of the world, *Ultima Thule* for the Olmec, must be represented by a boulder lying on the surface of a coffee plantation called Las Victorias, near Chalchuapa in western El Salvador. This boulder is carved on several surfaces with what seems to be the most simple and crude Olmec relief known, but the caped and helmeted figures are definitely Olmec.

Again the question might be asked: Why did the Olmec cross the Isthmus and establish posts down the Pacific Coast of Chiapas and Central America? Here I am speculating, but the answer I would again give is: jade. Some of the loveliest jades known for the Pre-Columbian New World have come from richly stocked graves in the Nicoya Peninsula of northwestern Costa Rica. Many of these objects happen to be of the same blue-green color so well known among the Olmec, and no small number (while not exactly in Olmec style) are identical to some jades found in Olmec sites in Guerrero and Veracruz. Two jade figures from Nicoya are, however, purely Olmec, showing bald, baby-faced individuals with bat-like wings; since this latter feature is not found elsewhere, it is likely that they were made locally in the peninsula. Until quite recently, nothing was known of the age of Nicoya jade. Archaeological excavations carried out in the area during 1960 by Dr. Claude Baudez of the Musée de l'Homme (Paris) and by myself have shown that there was an early occupation corresponding to the Late Formative of Mesoamerica. We now have evidence that Nicoya jades are at least as old as this, which would put them back in the centuries before the Christian Era. But I myself feel that many of them are far earlier, in fact coeval with at least the later part of the Olmec civilization (from 800 to 400 B.C.).

There is so much jade known for Nicoya that there must be a local source. My present idea is that the Olmec of the heartland knew of this and raided down to Costa Rica along the Pacific coastal plain, leaving military posts and their own monuments along the way.

In all of the expansion described in this chapter, they took more along with them than just their art style and commerce: they disseminated civilization itself, unknown before they appeared. Mesoamerica as we know it was really their creation. Where they did not go, or where their influence was unfelt, civilized life never took hold, not even in the two and a half millennia that elapsed between then and the Spanish conquest. Beyond the frontier of the Olmec realm were the barbarians, the people without calendar, writing, and science, without great art, without states and civilized centers. There is one strange exception to this picture, however: the Maya area. Setting aside one odd relief on a cliff in the wild Lacandon Indian country of Chiapas, there is no known Olmec monument in all of that region occupied later by the Classic Maya. Why should this be the case? A paradoxical solution will be suggested in the last chapter, namely, that the Olmec *were* the Maya.

7. RECONSTRUCTING OLMEC LIFE

One of the principal goals of prehistory is the reconstruction of past cultures and civilizations, not only their ways of making a living, but also their society, politics, thought, and religion. By following only one line of evidence, and proceeding full speed ahead without a general knowledge of the anthropology of civilizations, the archaeologist cannot hope to put back together the fragments that he has been left into a meaningful picture. Faulty reconstructions of this sort have been the butt of many cartoons.

In recent years human ecology, the many-faceted relationship between groups of men and their environments, has been among the most fruitful aspects of prehistory. One obvious way of studying ancient ecology is by looking at the peoples today who are living in the same area as the earlier population, provided, of course, that the environment has not changed radically and that the modern people are living on roughly the same economic level. It would do little good, for instance, to examine the modern suburbanites of Connecticut for clues as to how the Algonquian Indians of the same area once lived. Luckily for the archaeologist, many parts of the world in which he works and digs have been only lightly touched by the Industrial Revolution, and major climatic changes have not taken place since the demise of the cultures he wants to reconstruct.

And luckily for us, the tropical lowlands of southern Mexico, where the Olmec civilization arose, is such a region, not very much altered by the Machine Age. Side by side with our archaeological work at San Lorenzo Tenochtitlán,

A hunter with a deer, a long-standing protein source in the San Lorenzo area.

The variability of the tropical lowland area of three significant Olmec sites—San Lorenzo (the main site), Tenochtitlán, and Potrero Nuevo—is indicated by the map. The area surveyed, encompassing about 30 square miles, was used by the author and other scholars to study the present-day local ecology in order to reconstruct it for Olmec times. The key to economic and political power, now and in the past, is the highly productive land of the river levees.

we have been studying the local peasantry in the zone, prying into their kitchens, asking questions about farming, accompanying them on fishing expeditions, and diplomatically uncovering their social and political lives. We have two goals here. One is to discover, given native systems of agriculture and subsistence, the ultimate limit to the population which once lived in the environs of San Lorenzo Tenochtitlán; if this ultimate "carrying capacity" is substantially below that required to support the building, monument-hauling, and other public activities of these sites, then the area which supported them must have been very large, indeed, reaching well outside the zone.

The second goal is to understand not just the limits imposed upon the ancient and modern inhabitants by their wet, tropical surroundings, but also the very complex ways in which they adapt to that environment—and, of considerable importance, the ways in which that environment has been changed by them.

Ten or twenty years ago these ambitious goals would have been impractical. To get quantified data of this sort, one has to map soils, vegetation types, and land-use patterns. This task has been made immeasurably easier and quicker by aerial photography, which can carry out in an hour what it would have taken teams of scientists and surveyors months to accomplish on foot. Working for our project, a Mexican company specializing in photogrammetric mapping has flown over our sample area of some thirty square miles and has produced highly detailed photographs (on which even individual corn plants in native fields can be counted) and fine-scale maps from these. From such maps and from extensive field studies they have broken down the area into types of soils (some of which are unusable savanna lands), forest and grassland formations, and potential land use.

All this would mean little if these maps were not tied in with our own ethnological investigations, often conducted on week ends or by talking to our workmen while digging was in progress. We asked all sorts of questions, particularly how much corn, beans, and other crops are produced by a specified kind of soil, how much of this soil type must be left fallow, and for how long, and consumption figures per household and per person. Once these figures are coordinated with our photogrammetric maps, we can arrive at conclusions about maximum possible populations today, and by extrapolation, about populations three thousand years ago.

Our local farmers practice "shifting" or slash-and-burn cultivation, like many of the tropical peoples of the world. A patch of forest or bush is selected and felled with ax and machete during the dry season. Just before the great rains come (at the end of May or in early June), it is burned, and towering smoke columns darken the sky. Planting takes place after the first downpour, the corn seeds being dropped in holes made through the ashes with a simple digging stick. After one or more harvests, the plot (called *milpa*, a term used over much of Mesoamerica) is abandoned and allowed to revert to bush, that is, it lies fallow and gradually recovers its lost fertility. "Shifting" cultiva-

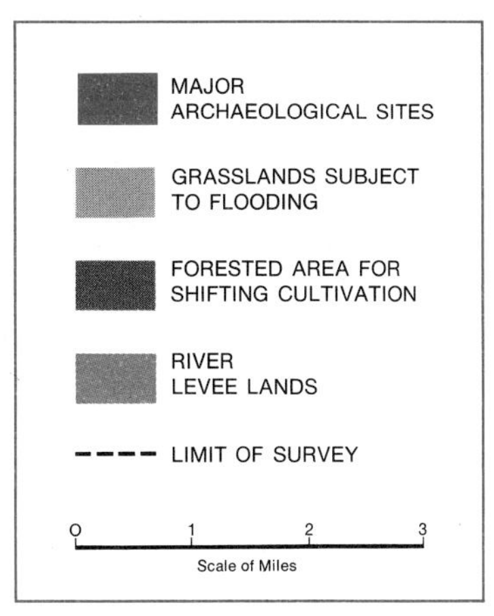

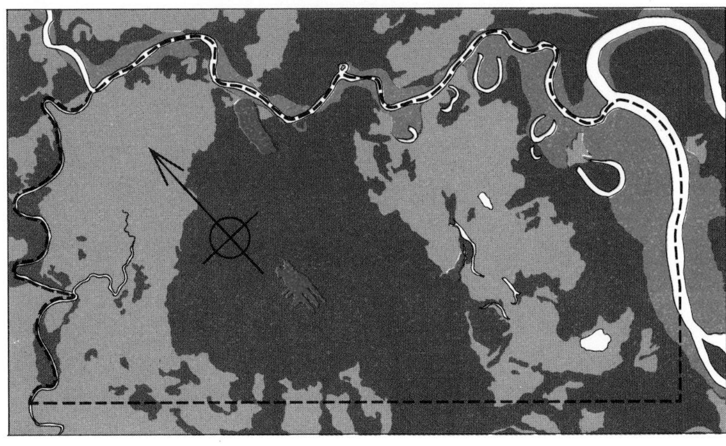

tion, because it demands a large fallow area, is thought by many scholars to be a poor base for the development of high cultures, compared with the more intensive and occasionally irrigated kinds of cultivation in use in more temperate or drier regions. The fact remains, however, that it supported the great Maya civilization of the Classic stage and probably provided the subsistence base of the Olmec, too. The question to ask is: How?

Local agriculture in the San Lorenzo Tenochtitlán area is no simple matter. It is very much more complex and productive than one would think at first glance. Once a year during the rainy season (from May until November) the rivers rise, swelled by tremendous thundershowers accompanied by savage lightning. All land lying below the 75-foot altitude line is inundated, and great sheets of water abounding in fish cover the low-lying savannas. The result is that the highly acid savanna soils are so heavy with clay and so poor in nutrients that they cannot be farmed at any time of year. Above the high-water mark, in the hillier zone, soils are good and can be cultivated throughout the year, with two major harvests. The really prime land, however, is, like the savannas, the gift of the floods: the natural levees along the rivers that are covered with a deep layer of rich silt after the waters recede. Although only a dry-season crop can be brought in, the corn yield is fantastic, as high as 3,200 pounds per acre as compared with 1,780 pounds for the hillier lands.

The lucky individual who has access to the levee lands need only cultivate three-quarters of an acre during only part of the year to support himself and his family, while the "upland" farmer, denied these soils, has to work at least an acre over the entire year. Small wonder, then, that while the uplands of the area belong to an *ejido* (a communal landholding unit), the lands along the river are all in private hands. In fact, it is possession of the latter which provides the local political and economic leaders with much of their power. We think that they must have given a similar power base to the Olmec leaders of 1000 B.C.

With all this data virtually at our fingertips, we can make some sort of estimate of the human carrying capacity of the zone. Subtracting the agriculturally unusable portion of the area, and allowing for the present average fallow period of eight to ten years, then our present thinking is that the upper limit of population must be about five thousand people. What this means for the reconstruction of Olmec politics we shall see.

Ninety per cent of what the modern villagers eat is corn, mainly prepared as tortillas. Fishing, hunting, and turtle-collecting provide important supplements to this dull diet, and they are carried out with the unsporting thoroughness that is typical of people who are looking for food rather than pleasure. Every week end dozens of hunters ride out to San Lorenzo with their dogs, returning to Tenochtitlán in the afternoon with white-tailed deer, the brown brocket (a diminutive and delicious tropical forest deer), and collared peccary, three creatures that also appear in the cuisine of the ancient Olmec.

Some of the basic nutrition sources for the people of the San Lorenzo Tenochtitlán area are depicted below: left, axogo, *resembling Indian corn of the U.S. and one of the six native varieties of corn that constitute 90 per cent of the local diet; top right, a common wild pig, the collared peccary; and below, a tropical gar, netted in one of the ponds of the low-lying savanna. It was just such food, scientists believe, that also supported the ancient Olmec.*

Fishing goes on all year, although the kinds of fish and ways of catching them change from season to season. The small ponds and oxbows that have been left out on the savannas by former meanderings of the river system teem with fish; in former times a poison extracted from a forest vine was used to kill them in quantities. In June and July, when the great floods come, huge tarpon and gar swim out across the savannas, pursued by the villagers in canoes brandishing harpoons and pronged spears. Toward the latter part of the rainy season, when the rivers are still high and turbid, the prime target is the snook, or robalo, a keen-eyed fish that must be netted at night from canoes, since it can see the net coming during the daylight. The robalo, which can reach great size, is the favored eating fish around San Lorenzo Tenochtitlán. It was so in the past, as well, for many of its bones have been identified by Dr. Elizabeth Wing of the University of Florida in Olmec debris from the San Lorenzo area.

So much for our studies of native subsistence patterns. What do they mean for the reconstruction of Olmec society and politics? Apparently, the support area for each Olmec center must have been very much larger than the thirty square miles we have taken as our base for San Lorenzo. There is additional information for La Venta that bears upon the subject. The island of La Venta, for instance, could only support some forty-five to fifty households under native conditions, even if all its land was available for farming, which it most certainly was not. A tract of land away from the swamps surrounding the island has been calculated as being able to contain a maximum population of sixteen thousand, but this figure is far too high, as the exact area of poor or unusable soils has not been taken into account.

It is too early to precisely define the actual territory subordinate to each Olmec center. But the man power called upon to support its activities, many of which seem to us extraordinarily wasteful, must have been truly formidable. Consider the size and weight of the monuments from San Lorenzo and La Venta. It took seventeen men to lift and transport the half-ton Monument 17 at San Lorenzo a mere two miles to the schoolhouse in Tenochtitlán. How many would it have required to drag the forty-ton Monument 14 from its quarrying place in the Tuxtla Mountains to a raft on a navigable stream, thence by waterways to the base of the San Lorenzo plateau, and from there up to the surface of the site? My guess is that at least two thousand able-bodied men would have been involved in the operation, representing the effective labor of a population of eight to ten thousand persons. There are now sixty of these monuments known for San Lorenzo Tenochtitlán (and chances are that hundreds more remain still to be discovered), which is about the same number as at La Venta, and more than twenty at Laguna de los Cerros, to mention only the most important Olmec centers.

Add to this the several thousand tons of imported serpentine blocks found at La Venta, the basalt columns at the same site, and the thirty tons of drain stones at San Lorenzo.

Then consider the work involved in building the top twenty-five feet of the San Lorenzo plateau and its ridges (with hundreds of thousands of tons of artificial fill) and the ceremonial center of La Venta (with its specially selected clays). The only possible conclusion is that the political power of each center was exerted many dozens of miles away from it, and that the force and authority of the Olmec were felt far beyond the heartland itself. Three thousand years ago, there just could not have been enough able-bodied men in the immediate area to have carried out all the physical labor required.

It has often been claimed that the Olmec civilization must have been a theocracy, defined as a government directed by priests, based on the analogy of the supposedly theocratic Maya. But this analogy will not work, since we can now interpret the historical part of some Classic Maya inscriptions. These speak to us of secular, rather than religious, leadership, with power in the hands of a hereditary lineage or dynasty. This conforms with what we know about all other Mesoamerican societies for which we have evidence. In these, the priesthood, while admittedly important, played second fiddle to the civil rulers.

The testimony of archaeology is that the Olmec were also ruled by great civil lords, members of royal lineages. As one line of evidence, let us take the so-called altars, those that show a figure seated cross-legged in a niche. Here there are only two themes: the person, an adult male in all cases, is holding a werejaguar baby in his arms, or else he is grasping a rope that is connected to two bound captives on the sides. These are surely the same themes of lineage (or descent) and personal conquest that have recently been identified on the Maya monuments, and they are intended to glorify the ruler to his subjects. The Colossal Heads are a case in point: enormous sculptures that so obviously depict tough warrior dynasts rather than priests. There is some suspicion that beside playing the dual role of king and soldier, the ruler was also an outstanding athlete (like Henry VIII and other European kings). From clay figurines found at San Lorenzo we know that the sacred ball game was played by the Olmec, and details both of posture and costume imply that many monuments celebrate prowess on the playing fields.

In the previous chapter it was shown that the Olmec had probably established a far-flung trading network reaching to the state of Guerrero in the west and to El Salvador in the southeast. The purpose of such conquests was perhaps to guarantee the export of jade and serpentine from their natural sources to great centers, and jade-hungry kings, in the Olmec heartland. Much, much later the Aztec conducted a similar kind of trade. This was in the hands of a hereditary mercantile group, called the *pochteca*, and was specifically designed to bring otherwise unobtainable luxury items to the Aztec royal palace. The pochteca traders operated exclusively in foreign territory, usually traveling disguised but well-armed over vast distances to obtain these items in special "ports of trade," looking for products like quetzal feathers, amber, jade, and gold. They

OVERLEAF: *A homestead in tiny Potrero Nuevo is the modern equivalent of another dwelling that stood on the same spot about 1000* B.C. *Thousands of years of human adaptation to the resources of the environment have produced a way of life that is largely self-sustaining. Seen in this one photograph are such direct reflections of Olmec life as the thatched roof of local palm fronds; the dip net used to snare shrimp in a lagoon beyond the trees; the living fence posts, which are one of several kinds of trees that regenerate after being set in the ground; the wooden trough used for washing food, clothes, and small children. (And in a garden behind the house grow numerous vegetables and flowers long native to the area.) Distinctly post-conquest, however, are the saw-cut wallboards, the barbed wire, the bucket, and the chicken, one of a multitude of domestic animals introduced to the New World with the Spaniards' arrival.*

were also *agents provocateurs*, an attack on them bringing quick retribution from the Aztec ruler in the form of bloody conquest. In fact, this was typically the way in which foreign countries were subjugated as tribute-producing provinces within the Aztec empire.

If the Aztec pattern can be projected back to the Olmec past, then the initial contacts might have been made by the pochteca under royal protection, with conquest and organization into the Olmec state falling shortly thereafter. Accepting all this as probable, then there must have been an Olmec empire (a thesis that has also been proposed by Alfonso Caso), the first of four that held sway over much of Mexico for fifteen centuries: Olmec, Teotihuacán, Toltec, and Aztec. It was typical of the later empires to have been governed from not just one, but two and sometimes three capitals. In the case of the Olmec, these might have been San Lorenzo, La Venta, and Laguna de los Cerros, with one and then the other in turn gaining ascendancy over the others.

Let us now turn to Olmec religion, for which there is much more direct evidence than for society and politics. It can be said with conviction that the major gods of Mesoamerica took on their forms and roles in Olmec times. The idea has been put forward several times, not only in this book but in others, that the great god of the Olmec was the werejaguar, a combination of feline features with those of a human baby, which is believed to have been an early form of the Rain God. Now this is indeed an oversimplification stemming from the little work that has been done on the iconography of the Olmec and later peoples. It is true that *one* of the werejaguars was the Rain God, the direct ancestor of Tlaloc among the Aztec and Chac among the Maya. He is equipped with the typical cleft head and snarling mouth, but his distinctive feature (differentiating him from other werejaguar gods) is a decorated, horizontal band above his forehead. Further, he is probably to be distinguished from another very similar monster who has a shoot of corn sprouting up from the cleft, obviously the Maize God of the Mesoamerican religions.

The clue to the identification of four other gods is a quite remarkable green stone statue discovered at Las Limas, Veracruz, in 1965 by two Indian boys. The figure shows a young male Olmec seated cross-legged, with a small werejaguar lying in his arms, the same motif already seen on some basalt altars. In this case, the little monster is certainly the Rain God. However, on the figure's shoulders and knees are incised four faces, each of which is a cleft-headed werejaguar in profile. The artist has taken great care to show that each head is different from the others, and from the creature in the lap. Two are easy to identify from what we already know about the significant features of the gods in later cultures.

On the right shoulder is the god Xipe, here with the double bands curving through his eye exactly as in the art of the Zapotec, Maya, and Aztec. Xipe was the Lord of Spring and of regeneration, impersonated by Aztec priests wearing the skins of flayed captives. On the left knee is depicted the Death God, with closed eyelid and fleshless upper jaw.

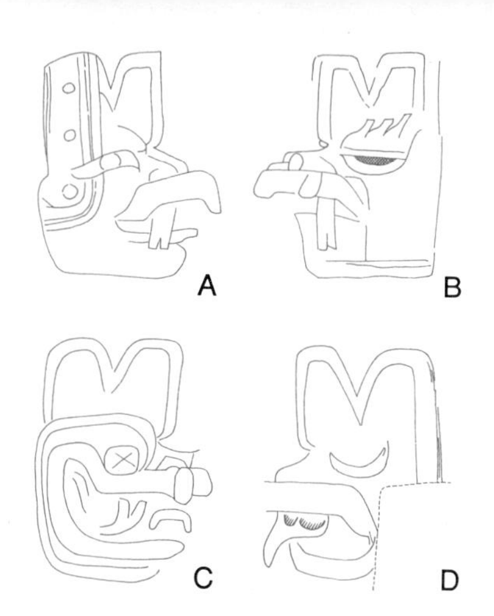

The drawings at left are of heads scratched on to the shoulders and knees of an Olmec figure found at Las Limas, Veracruz (see page 2). Drawn by the author, they depict, for the first time, four of five gods recently identified as the major deities of the Olmec: (A) Xipe, God of Springtime; (B) the Fire Serpent (who bears the sun across the sky) or possibly the Fire God (lord of volcanoes and the household hearth); (C) Quetzalcóatl, God of Wisdom and Life; (D) the

It is less easy to pin down the face on the left shoulder, but there is firm evidence that we have here the flame-browed head of the so-called Fire Serpent (actually a four-legged reptile) who was responsible for carrying the sun on its journey across the sky. This deity was in Mexican mythology the representative of another even more important being, the Fire God—master of the volcanoes and god of the domestic hearth. And on the right knee is the Feathered Serpent, with crossed bands in eye and squared nose indicating his avatar as Wind God.

There is a philosophy in the figure from Las Limas that is crying out for explanation, but for which we can only make guesses. Perhaps we have the ancient Mexican belief in the unity of opposite principles: Xipe and the Feathered Serpent standing for greenness and Life, opposed to the Fire Serpent—harbinger of heat and drought—and Death. That the world is not an exactly even balance of both is suggested by the primary position of the Rain God, bringer of good harvests. These, then, are the five first gods of ancient Mesoamerica. The interesting trait that both gods and men are impressed with the features of the jaguar might stem from an Olmec belief in that awesome animal as the "noble" beast. Among the later Maya of the Classic, there were important warrior dynasties whose names incorporated the hieroglyph for jaguar, and as has been stated, some modern Maya peoples identify their rulers with jaguars.

The Feathered Serpent (Quetzalcóatl among the Aztec, Kukulcán among the Maya) was the high god of the royal house in Post-Classic times, devotion to his cult occasionally being the prerogative of the dynasts themselves. A fairly easy-to-understand depiction of the god occurs on Monument 20 from La Venta (the priest-king seated in the snake's coils holding the incense bag sacred to Quetzalcóatl), the feathers being arranged in a ruff on the top of the head (as they are in the astonishing paintings of Juxtlahuaca). At San Lorenzo and on Petroglyph 5 at Chalcatzingo, the plumage appears as a little wing behind the head. Not only the plumes characteristic of the monster can be stylized to almost symbolic form, but also the snake motif itself. In Maya hieroglyphic writing, the sign for "sky" or "heaven" and that for "snake" are the same: a pair of crossed bands like an X within a cartouche. The reason is that in Maya the two words are near-homonyms (*caan* and *can*), the glyph originating from the crossed bands to be seen on the back of the fer-de-lance and rattlesnake.

So the Feathered Serpent could be indicated in symbolic fashion, by putting the crossed bands in his eye (this is why the "cave" in Petroglyph 1 at Chalcatzingo is the mouth of Quetzalcóatl) and/or adding feathers or a little wing. Likewise the Fire Serpent could be referred to simply by his flame brow, mouth, and/or hand, or Xipe by the bands through the eye. Much of the finest Olmec pottery from San Lorenzo, Tlatilco, and Las Bocas shows just this repertory of godly symbols. In a way, this is the first stage in the evolution of writing, one step beyond pictographs or depictions of complete objects to communicate; here, a part (that is, the markings on the back of a snake) stands

Death God. (The god not shown is the Rain God.) Since each deity is cast in the familiar werejaguar form, it now seems certain that the numerous were-jaguar figures discovered to date may not represent a single god, as was previously thought, but any one of the five—or more. This is a major new insight into the nature of the Olmec religion. At right, redrawn from a 16th-century codex, is the Feathered Serpent, Quetzalcóatl, a deity still being worshiped in Aztec times.

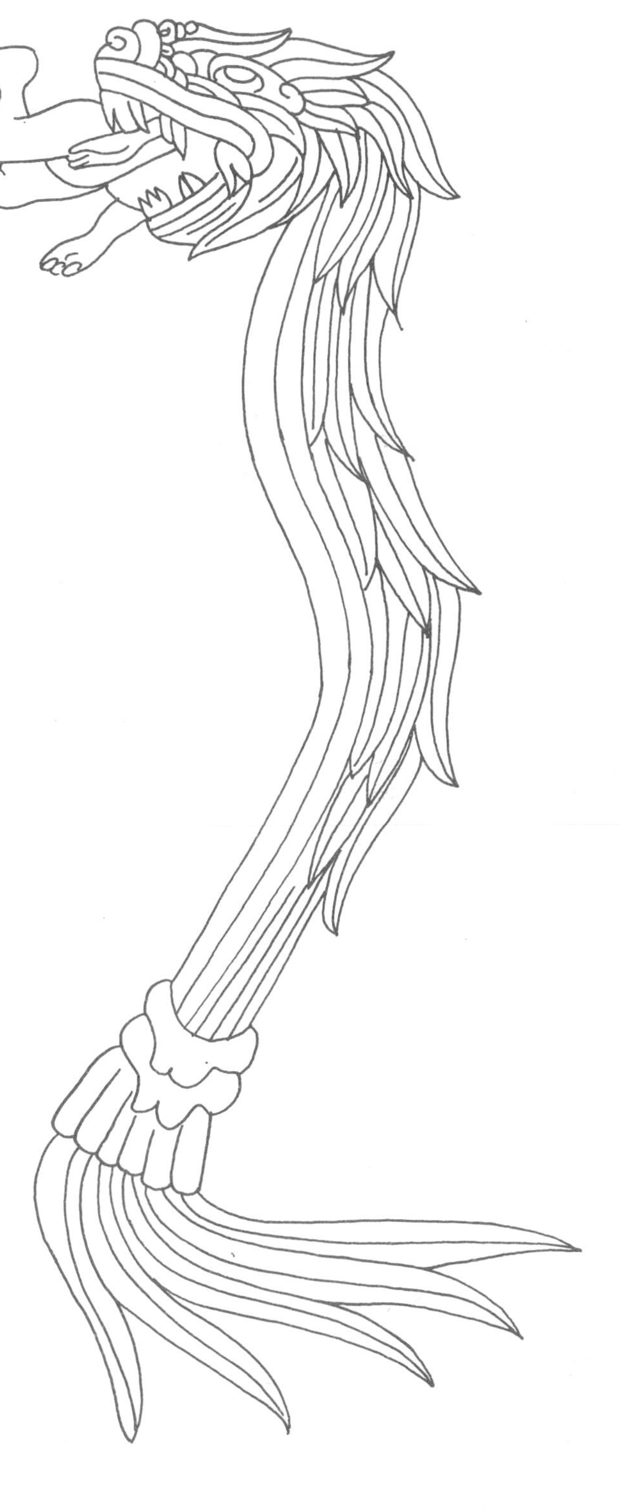

for the whole. It is possible that the Olmec wise men had books in which such an embryonic script was used. Another suggestion of at least a protoliteracy among the early Olmec is Monument 13 from La Venta, the so-called Ambassador (a Covarrubias drawing of it is on page 148). This shows a striding, bearded figure in relief carrying a standard. Behind him is a footprint, perhaps indicating his journey to or from somewhere, while arranged before him in a vertical row are three objects that certainly do look like glyphs—perhaps his name or ancestry.

At the same time, the Olmec must have been looking up at the sky and keeping track of the days and the annual passage of the sun to the north and back again. Because of its universality among the later Mesoamericans, surely they must have kept count of the ritual 260-day cycle, so basic to Mesoamerican religions. The Long Count does not, however, appear anywhere before 36 B.C.; by 31 B.C. the rulers of Tres Zapotes had ordered their now-famous Stela C to be carved. The very earliest Long Count dates appear in the Olmec area and scattered from there up to the Grijalva Valley of Chiapas and on the Pacific Coast of Guatemala away from the Maya area proper. This distribution implies that the best-known trait of Classic Maya civilization was not invented by the Maya but by some other people, perhaps by very late Olmec. But, it should be pointed out, we are here on very shaky grounds, for Olmec civilization as it is usually defined had surely been extinct for several centuries by the time that this highly advanced calendar came into existence.

8. ACHIEVEMENT AND LEGACY OF THE OLMEC

Who were the Olmec? What language did they speak? And by what name did they call their jungle-covered homeland? At first glance, it might be thought that these questions would be as unfathomable as the problem of what song the Sirens sang to Odysseus, since we are dealing with a people for whom we have no written documents who came to prominence over three thousand years ago—who were, in fact, contemporaries of that Greek hero. The solution, however, is far from hopeless insofar as the identification of the Olmec is concerned, but we here must turn to nonarchaeological evidence.

A key piece of data is the memory that the Mexican peoples had of their past, not only of the few centuries before the Spanish conquest, but of much more distant times. One such account recorded in the Náhuatl language by Father Sahagún opens with, "Behold the story which the old people told," and continues with the legendary arrival of the ancestors of the Mexican people from across the water. Making a landing in what is now northern Veracruz, they followed the coast line south. At last they came to a place called Tamoanchán. Among them were wise old men who had all the "writings, the books, the paintings" in their possession; then one day they left Tamoanchán carrying these and an image of their god with them. The people were left desolate, but four of the old men who had been left behind counseled together and decided to carry on the torch of civilization by themselves. "Then they devised the book of days [the 260-day count], the book of years, the count of the years, the book of

Tikal, hub of Maya civilization, culminates a way of life begun by the Olmec.

The map indicates the present distribution of the main body of Mayan languages in the Petén-Yucatán Peninsula, Guatemala, neighboring lands, and a lonely outlying group, Huastec, far up on the Gulf Coast. This, and the proximity of two linguistic relatives (Totonac and Mixe-Zoque) to the Olmec heartland, makes it virtually certain that all Mayan tongues were once found within the heartland and were dispersed after the breakup of the Olmec state.

dreams. . . ." Eventually Tamoanchán was abandoned. "And they departed . . . from Tamoanchán. Offerings were made at a place named Teotihuacán. And there all the people raised pyramids for the sun and for the moon."

There follow descriptions of the successive civilizations of Teotihuacán, Toltec Tula, and finally the founding of Aztec Tenochtitlán. Four successive states since the "distant past, which no one still can reckon," with Tamoanchán the earliest.

Because it was founded prior to the great city of Teotihuacán, Tamoanchán must have flourished in the Formative period. We would know a great deal more about it if the Aztec emperor Itzcóatl had not burned its history, a dictatorial act that he justified by saying: "It is not necessary for all the common people to know of the writings; government will be defamed, and this will only spread sorcery in the land; for it containeth many falsehoods."

A striking aspect of the Tamoanchán problem is that the name itself makes very little sense in the Aztec tongue (Sahagún gives a poor derivation from the Náhuatl *temooa tocha*, "we seek our home"). It makes a great deal of sense, however, in Mayan! *Ta* is the locative prefix meaning "at" or "in," very common in Mayan place names; *moan* was a mythical bird, the lord of the thirteenth layer of heaven; *chan* is an archaic form of *can* or *caan*, indicating both "snake" and "sky." Therefore, among the Mayan-speaking peoples of southern Mesoamerica, Tamoanchán most likely would be interpreted as the Land of the Bird-Snake—that is, of the Feathered Serpent. At the same time, since Mayan is a language full of homonyms and therefore of double meanings, Tamoanchán could also be read as Land of the Rainy Sky.

Granting, then, that Tamoanchán was the name of the first civilized state in ancient Mesoamerica; that these people spoke some form of Mayan; that the Feathered Serpent was a deity of great importance among them; and that their land was rainy—does this not lead us directly to the Olmec civilization of the southern Gulf Coast? Linguistics has something to add to this. The Mayan language family includes some twenty-seven mutually unintelligible tongues, all, however, closely related to each other. As the linguistic map shows, all but one of them are concentrated in the Petén-Yucatán Peninsula and the neighboring highlands of Chiapas and Guatemala. This one lone outpost is Huastec, spoken today in the hills above the northern Gulf Coast, in the states of Tamaulipas, far northern Veracruz, and San Luis Potosí; towns along the Pan-American Highway were once Huastec-speaking.

At one point in time, Huastec must have been contiguous with the other Mayan languages, and then became separated. There are three possibilities to explain this, of which the first two are unlikely: all of the other Mayan languages were once in Huastec country, but departed en masse, leaving Huastec behind; the ancestral Huastec lived in what is now the Maya area proper, but left by themselves for the northwest; or all of the Mayan tongues were once found together in an intermediate zone, Huastec subsequently moving to its present position and the others to the east, into the

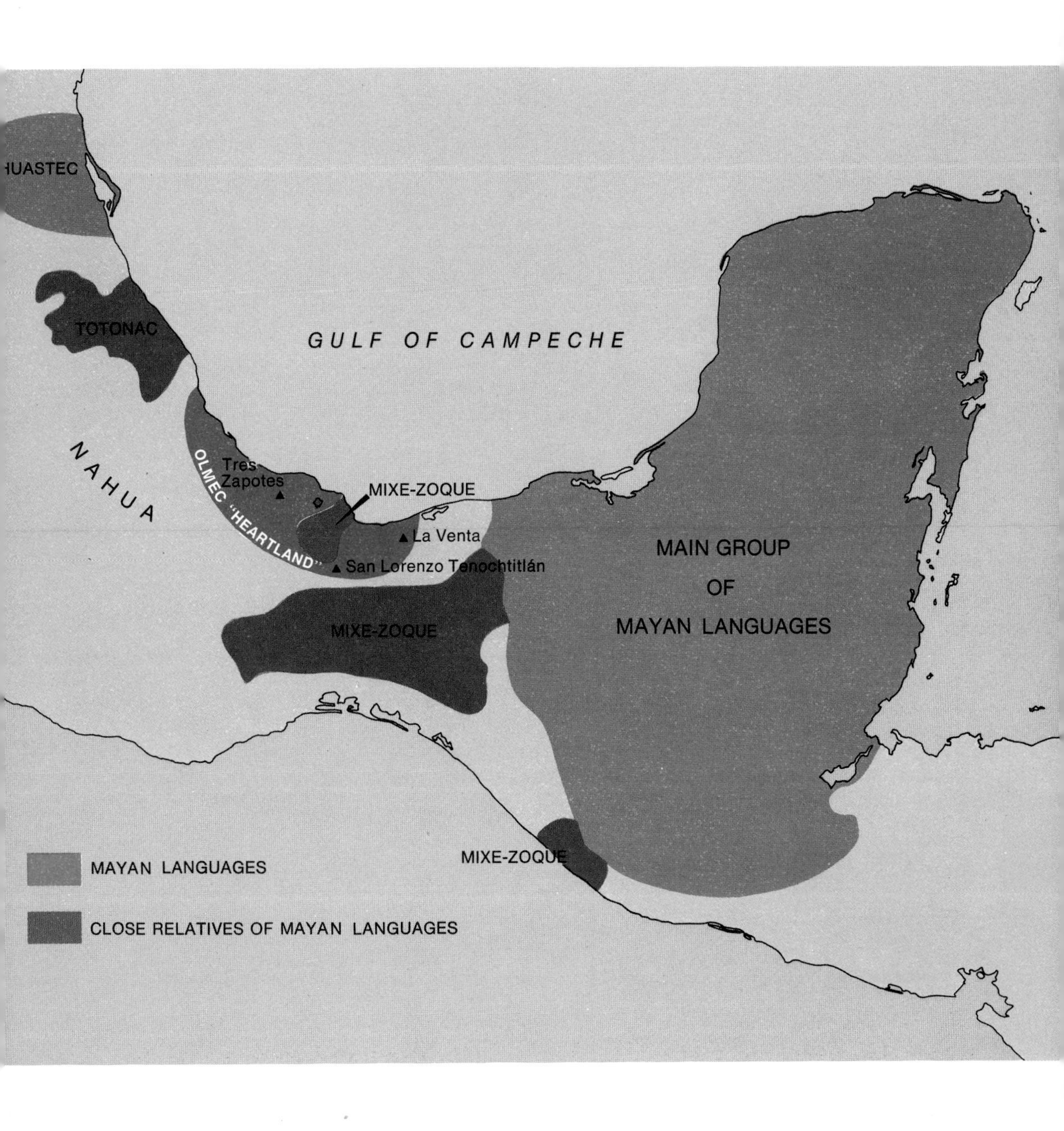

HUASTEC
TOTONAC
GULF OF CAMPECHE
NAHUA
OLMEC "HEARTLAND"
Tres Zapotes
MIXE-ZOQUE
La Venta
San Lorenzo Tenochtitlán
MAIN GROUP OF MAYAN LANGUAGES
MIXE-ZOQUE
MIXE-ZOQUE
MAYAN LANGUAGES
CLOSE RELATIVES OF MAYAN LANGUAGES

The oldest part of the Zapotec center of Monte Albán (below, left), one of the most impressive sites in Mesoamerica, is the Court of the Danzantes with its strange stone slabs (right). The crude relief figures—eyes closed, mouths gaping, bodies contorted—most likely depict slain enemy rulers. Olmec influence is apparent in the characteristic drooping mouths. Here, as elsewhere in Mesoamerica, the older an art form, the closer it is to the Olmec.

present lowlands and highlands of the Maya area. The closest languages affiliated with the Mayan family are Totonac and Mixe-Zoque, the former on the northern border of the Olmec heartland, the latter near or actually within it. This suggests that ancestral Mayan was once located in the intermediate zone, that is, within the Olmec heartland of the southern Gulf Coast. If so, then it was probably the language of Tamoanchán. The departure of Mayan speakers would have left a vacuum to be filled by Mixe-Zoque and by Náhuatl.

A recent development within linguistics, called lexicostatistics or glottochronology, uses vocabulary comparison to assign dates to the divergence of related languages. By this method, the splitting off of Huastec from the other Mayan languages took place some three thousand years ago—that is, at a time when Olmec civilization was flourishing at San Lorenzo and La Venta. Sahagún tells us that the Huastec were expelled from Tamoanchán because their ruler, like Noah, had disrobed while intoxicated, casting off his breechclout in public. As the Olmec state (or states) began falling apart, first at San Lorenzo and later at La Venta, other Mayan groups began moving east, into the forested lands of the Petén-Yucatán Peninsula, and some up the river valleys into the oak- and pine-covered mountains of Chiapas and Guatemala.

What had once been the Olmec civilization eventually transformed itself into the Maya civilization. By the Late Formative, instead of the three-dimensional sculptural style that had typified the Olmec, we have the flat stelae decorated with baroque, narrative reliefs that are later to characterize the Classic Maya. This is the style which has been called Izapan, named for the key site of Izapa, on the Pacific Coast plain of southeastern Mexico, very near the Guatemala border. The Late Formative art of Izapa is obviously transitional between Olmec and the earliest known art of the Maya of northern Guatemala, where Maya civilization began to take shape after the time of Christ. Among the traits which the Izapan artists passed on to the Classic Maya is the stela-altar complex, in which a round altar is placed in front of a flat, upright slab embellished with the deeds of present or past rulers.

Along with other imported cultural items, the Long Count calendar appears in the center of the Maya lowlands (the Petén jungles of Guatemala and neighboring portions of the Yucatán Peninsula, British Honduras, and Honduras) by the end of the third century after Christ. But a great deal of the brilliant Classic Maya civilization of A.D. 300–900 is unparalleled elsewhere in Mesoamerica. In their new land, the Maya found a wealth of easily worked limestone for building, and at great sites like Tikal stone architecture based upon the principle of the corbel (or false) arch may appear even before the beginning of the Christian Era. The eventual result of this structural creativity was the towering temple-pyramid, of which six are known at Tikal (one is over two hundred feet high). Classic Maya art, particularly wall painting and relief sculpture, becomes incredibly refined and realistic, and it is difficult to believe, looking at this alone, that the style and its iconography could have had Olmec roots.

No few sentences can do justice to the achievement of the Maya in advancing the knowledge of astronomy and mathematics. Sophisticated calculations concerning the moon and eclipses, and determinations of the exact length of the year, appear in their surviving books and in part on their stone monuments. But what makes the Maya even more outstanding was that they alone among all the native peoples of the New World were fully literate; that is, they had a script sufficiently developed so they could write down *anything* in their language. This script has not yet been fully deciphered (only the calendrical portion can be read with certainty), but some remarkable advances have been made in recent years which show that the majority of the hieroglyphic texts on stelae and reliefs in the Classic centers record historical events, mainly births, marriages, and conquests among royal dynasts.

The Classic Maya civilization fell to ruin around A.D. 900. Archaeologists have no very firm answers as to why and how this happened, but there is ample evidence that a Toltec or Toltec-influenced people were pushing into the central Maya area from the Gulf Coast of Mexico and invading the remaining Maya centers at this time. Perhaps they were but a symptom, not a cause, of the downfall that may have been from internal revolt. At any rate, the Classic centers were abandoned, not to be revealed again in their jungle strongholds until Stephens, Catherwood, and other early explorers brought them to the light of modern scholarship.

Surely other Mesoamerican civilizations that took shape in the Formative stage owed a cultural debt to these Olmec innovators of the legendary Tamoanchán, such as the Zapotec of Oaxaca. Their great site of Monte Albán occupies a commanding position on a hilltop in the Valley of Oaxaca, in southern Mexico. Lining the basalt platform of one of the earliest temples known at Monte Albán are the Danzantes, numerous reliefs that show human figures depicted with a strange barbarity, arms and legs akimbo, mouths open and eyes closed, which is meant to tell the beholder that they are slain enemy chiefs. But significant here is that the Danzantes, the oldest art known for the Zapotec, are under strong Olmec influence, especially in the treatment of the faces, which show the drooping Olmec mouth. Already these ancient Zapotec, perhaps as early as the fifth century B.C., were writing, and hieroglyphic signs appearing on the Danzantes may be the names of the dead chiefs or kings. In fact, the Zapotec may have had even more to do with the invention of Mesoamerican scripts than the Olmec.

There is a steady development of Zapotec civilization out of that represented by the Danzantes. By the Classic stage, Monte Albán and other centers were mighty centers, perhaps even large towns, with control over many of Oaxaca's rich, irrigated valleys. And, as with the Maya, the later one gets in the Classic, the less obvious their debt to the Olmec becomes. The famous funerary urns and the murals of Classic Zapotec tombs bear little resemblance to either the style of the Danzantes or to the

OVERLEAF: *The most advanced stage of New World civilization, the Late Classic Maya, was probably best summed up in the jungles of southeastern Mexico, at Palenque. (The ruins pictured are those of the Temple of the Inscriptions.) The Olmec attitude toward form, and perhaps their vision of life, had become so changed by time that no Olmec influence is apparent. But that the high mark reached at Palenque began with, and was possible only because of, the Olmec, is now a certainty.*

rich Olmec art that influenced it. But any trip back in time in Mesoamerica takes one to the Olmec in one way or another.

As for Teotihuacán and central Mexico, we have the testimony of Sahagún's informants that an elite group from Tamoanchán founded that city. More prosaically, the rapid rise of Teotihuacán and its dominance of most of Mesoamerica during the Early Classic (A.D. 300–600) clearly owes its cause to the practice of irrigation agriculture in the great basin of the Valley of Mexico, and more particularly to control by Teotihuacán of the *chinampas* (intensively cultivated and watered garden plots) in the southern part of the great lake. The gods of Teotihuacán, like those of other Mesoamerican cultures, were born in the Olmec heartland, but Teotihuacán art and architecture have different, unknown roots.

Most archaeologists do not believe, as did Sahagún's old men, that the Olmec came from across the Atlantic, or even the Pacific, but the ultimate origins of this first New World civilization remain in doubt. If their civilization had never been discovered, the "steady evolution" model for the rise of civilization—from gradually cumulative steps toward man's control of his environment and its resources—would look valid. Unfortunately, present evidence indicates that the Olmec appeared upon the scene as an already evolved culture by 1200 B.C. A way out of the dilemma might be taken by some by denying that Olmec culture *was* a civilization, that it was only a "chiefdom." Be that as it may, almost all scholars are agreed that chiefdoms are internally ranked but classless societies in which the ruled are members of a single tribal group organized solely on the principles of kinship. They are also in accord that a civilization is a class society organized as a state, that is, with a power superordinate over the diverse tribal, ethnic, and class elements that are found within its borders.

There is every reason to think that there was a state organization among these ancient Olmec. Within the heartland, where a dominant role may have been played by the Mayan-speaking element, the monuments and tomb offerings testify to a great social differentiation between rulers and ruled. But much more significant is the clear-cut extension of Olmec power far beyond the borders of its tiny heartland outlined in the preceding chapters. We find expansions of this sort only among the attested political empires of later times, such as the Toltec and Aztec. There were not only classes but many ethnic groups subsumed by the sovereign might of the great Olmec centers, extending from coast to coast and down into lower Central America. No chiefdom could have accomplished this. Thus, there *was* an Olmec state, and the Olmec were civilized.

We know them to have been one of the "pristine" civilizations of the world, early states for which there are no local precedents simply because they were the first in their respective areas. Many of these constitute a puzzle, since they, like the Olmec, spring suddenly upon the scene without obvious antecedents. Of course, they must already have had an economy that would have provided a basis for state development. In the case of the Olmec, this base was

definitely the incredibly productive, Nile-like agriculture carried out along the river levees of the Coatzacoalcos River drainage. Economic power means political power, as we can see in San Lorenzo Tenochtitlán today, where the few individuals who control the villages are the same as those who control the river levee lands. Nonetheless, there is nothing in an advanced subsistence level which will guarantee that civilization will necessarily arise in a particular place. Among the Pre-Columbian chiefdoms of lower Central America, where the agricultural level was about the same as in many parts of Mesoamerica, the state never did appear.

It might be instructive to compare some of these pristine civilizations, particularly the ones with some kind of written records, both with each other and with what precedes and follows them. Such civilizations might be China under the Shangs, early Dynastic Egypt, Sumerian Mesopotamia, the early Khmer empire of Cambodia, and possibly even Benin of West Africa. It is characteristic of all of these that regardless of the contrast that has been made between states and the pre-existing tribally organized chiefdoms, the modes and quantity of production often do not appreciably differ between the two. A further point of coincidence is that the kinship principle does not die out with the advent of states: lineages and clans maintain a vigorous existence within the state. In fact, it is upon the building blocks of blood lines that the state organization is constructed, the royal line being but the first among many. As with the modern kingdoms of Europe, state power can be advanced by royal marriages linking groups as well as by warfare. In other words, in the primitive state, kinship is not canceled out by territoriality, as early scholars like Sir Henry Maine have maintained: for examples we can point to the clan-like "nomes" of Egypt or to the patrilineal clans of ancient China.

Subsistence and technology are therefore a precondition (obviously, Olmec culture would never have existed if plants such as corn had not been domesticated in the Archaic stage) but not a necessary cause of the rise of civilization. Much has been made of the irrigation systems of early Mesopotamia and Peru as an efficient cause of the rise of the state in those areas —the idea behind this "hydraulic theory" being that the controls necessary for building and maintaining the canals and distributing the water would necessitate a state apparatus. But Dr. Robert M. Adams of the University of Chicago has shown that the Mesopotamian state was in existence *before* irrigation, and recent information from highland Peru suggests the same thing.

This simply points up the importance of the "why" of the state. It also implies that ideological factors, perhaps even a modicum of choice, transformed some ancient chiefdoms into pristine civilizations. (This happened twice in the aboriginal New World: once in Peru after 1000 B.C., when the Chavín civilization appears, and once in Mesoamerica, with the arrival of the Olmec civilization after 1200 B.C. These events, by the way, may not be unconnected, since some archaeologists see Olmec influence in the art of Chavín.) What if some pre-

San Lorenzo chief had decided that he wanted monuments carved in basalt to glorify himself and his distinguished ancestors? What if he felt that these monuments should rest on a specially constructed, hill-like plateau that could be seen for miles? He would have to reach out beyond his own tribal domain, by conquest if necessary, to gain access to the basalt. He would have to organize the people within his new territory to do the work necessary. At hand was enough food with which to feed and pay those working for his embryonic state. As in time his chiefly lineage transformed itself into a dynasty, the social and ceremonial needs of the Olmec power became even more difficult to fulfill on the Gulf Coast, and the conquests of more distant regions began. Again, the army was supported by sufficient quantities of transportable food, exactly as the chinampas made it possible for the much later Aztec armies to subjugate Mexico on full stomachs.

Once a commitment of this sort had been made, there may have been no going back. Civilization is a self-addicting drug, as those backward peoples of the modern age who have been hooked on unnecessary luxuries such as wrist watches and transistor radios could testify. The disease of civilization spreads, either forcefully or because neighboring peoples are brought into trading or social relations with the dominant power. The move from a chiefdom to a state is thus a sudden quantum jump, rather than a slow evolution.

A final characteristic of the pristine civilizations, Olmec included, is their extraordinary vitality. It is as though the artists, architects, craftsmen, and people in general had no idea of their own limitations. The sheer amount of work done by the Olmec, for instance, staggers the imagination. Similarly, the huge pyramids of Egypt were erected at the beginning of the Nile civilization, not later. But it is the power and excitement of their art styles that most impress the twentieth-century observer. There is never anything again quite as overwhelmingly beautiful in Peruvian art as the reliefs of Chavín, nothing in Chinese art like the Shang bronzes, nor certainly anything in Mesoamerican art as great as Olmec. The inspiration was one of sheer creativity, for much of what they were doing had never been done before, at least among peoples with whom they were in communication. The pattern once established, later cultures could only embellish and elaborate upon it. If it were not for the periodic incursions of new and barbaric peoples into the old, civilized regions (this happened not only in Europe and Asia but many times over in Mesoamerica), these patterns would soon have become exhausted.

Our debt to people like the Olmec is profound. Countries like modern Mexico draw upon a rich pre-Spanish heritage that originated with the Olmec civilization, just as we Americans are legatees of a European-Mediterranean heritage that goes back to the Sumerians, Egyptians, Greeks, and Etruscans. We may be captives of history, but we are also its children. America's first civilization is part of the heritage of us all, speaking to us across the gulf of centuries with its message of human creativity and achievement.

One of the most famous relics of Aztec civilization is this calendar, which represents the Mesoamerican concept of time and the universe. A stone disk 12 feet in diameter, its center is the sun, carried across the sky by the Fire Serpents that encircle the rim. The ring of 20 symbols denotes the days of each month in the 18-month Aztec year. The signs around the sun depict the first four epochs of the earth. The Aztec were in the fifth epoch when Mesoamerican civilization was utterly destroyed.

APPENDIX

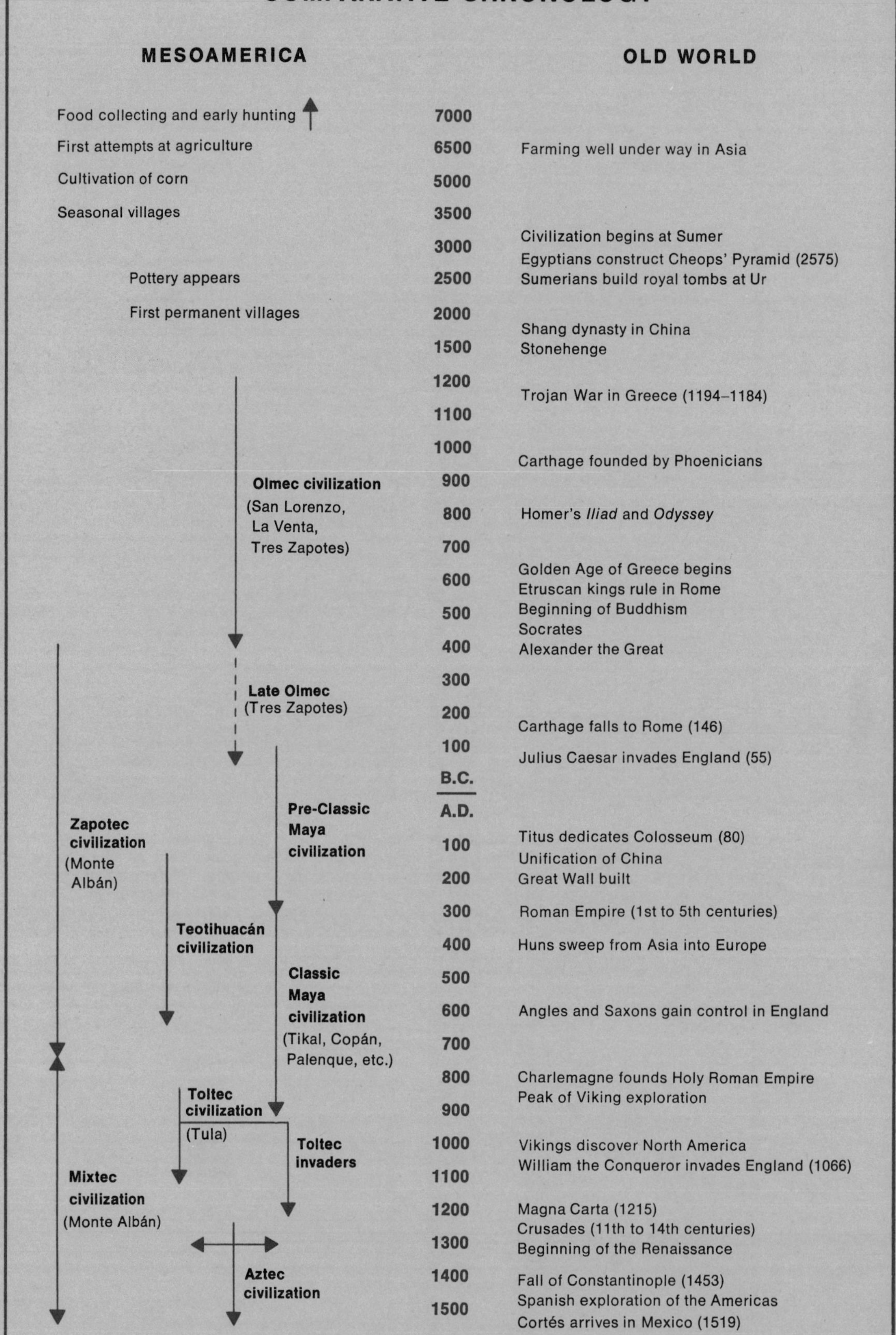
COMPARATIVE CHRONOLOGY
MESOAMERICA
OLD WORLD
Food collecting and early hunting
7000
First attempts at agriculture
6500
Farming well under way in Asia
Cultivation of corn
5000
Seasonal villages
3500
Civilization begins at Sumer
3000
Egyptians construct Cheops' Pyramid (2575)
Pottery appears
2500
Sumerians build royal tombs at Ur
First permanent villages
2000
Shang dynasty in China
1500
Stonehenge
1200
Trojan War in Greece (1194–1184)
1100
1000
Carthage founded by Phoenicians
Olmec civilization
(San Lorenzo,
La Venta,
Tres Zapotes)
900
800
Homer's *Iliad* and *Odyssey*
700
Golden Age of Greece begins
600
Etruscan kings rule in Rome
500
Beginning of Buddhism
Socrates
400
Alexander the Great
300
Late Olmec
(Tres Zapotes)
200
Carthage falls to Rome (146)
100
Julius Caesar invades England (55)
B.C.
A.D.
Pre-Classic
Maya
civilization
Zapotec
civilization
(Monte
Albán)
100
Titus dedicates Colosseum (80)
Unification of China
200
Great Wall built
300
Roman Empire (1st to 5th centuries)
Teotihuacán
civilization
400
Huns sweep from Asia into Europe
Classic
Maya
civilization
(Tikal, Copán,
Palenque, etc.)
500
600
Angles and Saxons gain control in England
700
800
Charlemagne founds Holy Roman Empire
Toltec
civilization
(Tula)
900
Peak of Viking exploration
Toltec
invaders
1000
Vikings discover North America
Mixtec
civilization
(Monte Albán)
1100
William the Conqueror invades England (1066)
1200
Magna Carta (1215)
Crusades (11th to 14th centuries)
1300
Beginning of the Renaissance
Aztec
civilization
1400
Fall of Constantinople (1453)
1500
Spanish exploration of the Americas
Cortés arrives in Mexico (1519)

NEWS FROM THE NEW WORLD

This series of excerpts comes from the writings of six men—a priest, a soldier of fortune, an explorer, and three archaeologists—who played decisive roles in the discovery of Mesoamerican civilizations. The accounts are arranged in historical time sequence, advancing from the sixteenth century to the 1960's, but the story they tell actually goes back in time—from the Aztec way of life at the time of the conquest to the origin of domestic corn, more than three thousand years before the birth of Christ.

For the Aztec, war was a way of life. They fought, not to kill, but to take captives who would later be sacrificed to their gods in elaborate and bloody rituals. Tezcatlipoca (above), their chief god, had originally been a Toltec deity. In incorporating him into their pantheon, the Aztec gave him the additional role of Lord of the Night Sky, who watched all their actions in a mirror made of obsidian. Hence his name, which translates from Náhuatl as Smoking Mirror.

THE SPANIARDS MARCH INTO MEXICO

Fortunately for history, the first Europeans to explore the New World were not all conquerors. The conquistadors were accompanied by priests, a few of whom tempered missionary zeal with a desire to chronicle the Indian civilizations that were being so brutally and instantly destroyed. One of the most remarkable of these was Bernardino de Sahagún, a Franciscan friar who came to Mexico in 1529. His profound knowledge of the Náhuatl language used by the Aztec enabled him to compile a massive 12-volume encyclopedia of Mexico, written in Náhuatl, the last volume of which covers the conquest itself, as seen through Aztec eyes.

The following extract describes the Spaniards' march on the chief city of the Aztec empire, Tenochtitlán (now Mexico City), whose people were paralyzed by fear that the advancing strangers were the bearded, white-skinned god Quetzalcóatl and his retinue. According to legend, the god was expected to return from exile to re-establish his rule in the year of his birth—which recurred in a 52-year cycle. Just such a year was 1519, when Hernán Cortés landed with a force of 600 men, some of them mounted on 16 magical animals that the Indians—who had never seen horses—could only describe as deer. They countered the Indians' stone-tipped weapons with steel swords, guns that belched smoke, and cannon that could topple walls. They were encased in armor that the natives took to be padded cotton like their own—until they saw the strangers emerge from battle practically unscathed. The Aztec legend was truer than they knew.

And upon this, here in Mexico, all lay quiet; [the people] did not go out or venture forth. Mothers did not let [children] go out. The roads were empty, and clear; the roads were clean, as in early morning. None crossed others' paths—they did not dare; they retired to their houses only to know that there was woe. The common folk said: "Pay no heed. Let [the hour] be accursed. What will you do? For now we shall die; we shall perish. Yea, now we await our death."

Accompanied by fife and drum (in the stern of the rear boat), Spanish troopships set sail from Cuba. Cortés' 11 small ships held an average of 55 men apiece, which made them almost as jammed as the tiny vessels pictured here. This engraving was made to illustrate the first publication, in 1522, of Cortés' letters informing the king of Spain of the conquest of the Aztec empire.

. . . And thereupon [the Spaniards] set out in order now to enter here into Mexico. Wherefore they prepared and arrayed themselves for war. They girt themselves and bound on their battle dress. Then the horse[men] were, each one, disposed, arranged in rows, placed in order, and put in line.

And the four horse[men] who came guiding, preceding, and moving ahead of the others and occupying the vanguard, were the leaders. They kept turning; they moved back and forth repeatedly; they went on, facing people. They looked hither and thither; they went on to scan every side and to look everywhere, peering among groups of houses. They proceeded examining everything. They kept looking up at the housetops. . . .

By himself came as guide, going as leader—going ahead alone—one who bore the standard upon his shoulders. He proceeded, waving it back and forth, making it circle, and tossing it from side to side. . . .

Following him passed the bearers of iron swords. Bared were their iron swords, which flashed brightly. They each bore and carried upon their shoulders their shields—wooden and leather shields.

The second group, the second file to come, was of horses carrying upon their backs many [soldiers] in their cotton armor cuirasses, each with leather shield and iron lance; and all with their iron swords hanging down the flanks of the horses. All had rattles; they had clatterers; they galloped along jingling, and the rattles clacked and resounded. The horses—the deer—neighed and whinnied. They sweated profusely; it was as if water fell from them. And flecks of foam fell in drops upon the ground; it dripped like soap[suds]. And as they advanced, great was the clangor and pounding of their hooves; the feet beat as when one casteth stones, and then they pierced holes and made depressions in the ground where they raised their feet. . . .

The third group was of those who bore iron crossbows. In their arms rested the crossbows. They came wielding and repeatedly testing them, sighting along them. . . . And their quivers went hung at their sides or passed under their arms; [these] went filled, crammed, with arrows—with iron bolts. Their cotton armor reached to their knees; it was very thick, very hard, very dense, like limestone. And their heads were likewise wrapped in cotton armor, and from the tops of their heads arose quetzal plumes, dividing and outspread.

The fourth group likewise was of horse[men], similar in array to what hath been told.

The Spaniards were appalled by the Aztec custom of human sacrifice. To the Indians, however, the role of victim was an honorable one, since it ensured a glorious afterlife. Stoically, those chosen to die would mount the steps of the temple of Huitzilopochtli, the Aztec God of War. At the top, each in turn was stretched over the sacrificial stone while a priest opened his chest with an obsidian knife and drew out the still-beating heart—a scene vividly depicted in this Indian drawing made soon after the Spanish conquest ended the rite.

The fifth group were those bearing harquebuses. . . . And when they had come into the great palace, the residence of the rulers, they fired them—they repeatedly shot the harquebuses. Now they each shattered [the air], they all crackled, scattering [the shot], and barked and thundered. Smoke was spread and diffused; it was dark with smoke. The fumes covered all the ground; they spread all over the soil. By its fetid smell it stupefied and robbed one of one's senses.

And at the very last came, directing from the rear, the greatest warrior, who was like the commanding general, experienced as war ruler and commander of warriors. Surrounding him, crowding about him, at his side and behind, went his brave warriors, his standard bearers, those who served him. . . .

Then all the dwellers in cities beyond the mountains . . . [the Spaniards' native allies] sped along at the rear. They came girt for war, with their cotton armor, their shields, their bows; their quivers filled and crammed with feathered arrows, some of barbed, wooden points, some blunted, some with obsidian points. They came crouching, and as they went, loosed cries and shrieks while striking their mouths with their hands; they screeched and whistled, and shook their heads.

And some bore burdens upon their backs; they carried rations on their backs. Some carried things [held by a tump line about] their foreheads, or some, their breasts; some bore things on carrying frames, some in cage-like baskets, some in deep, reed baskets; some bore bundles . . . upon their backs; some dragged the great lombard guns, which rested upon wooden wheels. And they moved them along shouting.

THE WONDERS OF TENOCHTITLAN

Hernán Cortés was born in Spain in 1485 to a family of poor country gentry. Originally intended for the law, he chose instead to seek his fortune in the newly established Spanish colonies in the New World. He arrived there in 1504, quickly acquired much influence, and, in 1518, was picked to command an expedition sent out from Cuba to explore the coast of Yucatán.

In March he landed in Tabasco, and after some hard-fought battles, formally took possession of the land in the name of Emperor Charles V. Sailing northward along the coast, he put ashore on Good Friday, 1519, at the spot where he was to build his first settlement: Villa Rica de Vera Cruz. There he was met by Moctezuma's ambassadors, bearing good-will offerings that seemed ample evidence of the country's wealth. These treas-

The Spanish cannon or lombards were probably falconets, which could be used aboard ship, as in the engraving on page 132, or mounted on wheels, as at left. To besiege the lake city of Tenochtitlán, shown at right in a map drawn in 1524 under Cortés' own supervision, the captain built a fleet of small ships, placing some of his precious cannon on board. The Aztec, in canoes, fled before the magic weapons, and the Spaniards then cut the causeways that were the city's life lines.

ures were loaded onto a ship, along with a letter to the king giving an account of the expedition's experiences, and the vessel set sail for Spain. Cortés then scuttled the remainder of his fleet and marched his little band westward, to conquer Mexico. The captain's second letter to Charles V, written after Moctezuma and his capital had been captured by the Spaniards, tells of the wonders of Tenochtitlán.

The great city of Tenochtitlán is built in the midst of this salt lake, and it is two leagues from the heart of the city to any point on the mainland. Four causeways lead to it, all made by hand and some twelve feet wide. The city itself is as large as Seville or Córdova. The principal streets are very broad and straight, the majority of them being of beaten earth, but a few and at least half the smaller thoroughfares are waterways along which they pass in their canoes. . . .

The city has many open squares in which markets are continuously held and the general business of buying and selling proceeds. One square in particular is twice as big as that of Salamanca and completely surrounded by arcades where there are daily more than sixty thousand folk buying and selling. Every kind of merchandise such as may be met with in every land is for sale there, whether of food and victuals, or ornaments of gold and silver, or lead, brass, copper, tin, precious stones, bones, shells, snails, and feathers; limestone for building is likewise sold there, stone both rough and polished, bricks burnt and unburnt, wood of all kinds and in all stages of preparation. . . . There is nothing to be found in all the land which is not sold in these markets, for over and above what I have mentioned there are so many and such various other things that on account of their very number and the fact that I do not know their names, I cannot now detail them. Each kind of merchandise is sold in its own particular street and no other kind may be sold there: this rule is very well enforced. All is sold by number and measure, but up till now no weighing by balance has been observed. A very fine building in the great square serves as a kind of audience chamber where ten or a dozen persons are always seated, as judges, who deliberate on all cases arising in the market and pass sentence on evildoers. In the square itself there are officials who continually walk amongst the people inspecting goods exposed for sale and the measures by which they are sold, and on certain occasions I have seen them destroy measures which were false.

There are a very large number of mosques or dwelling places for their

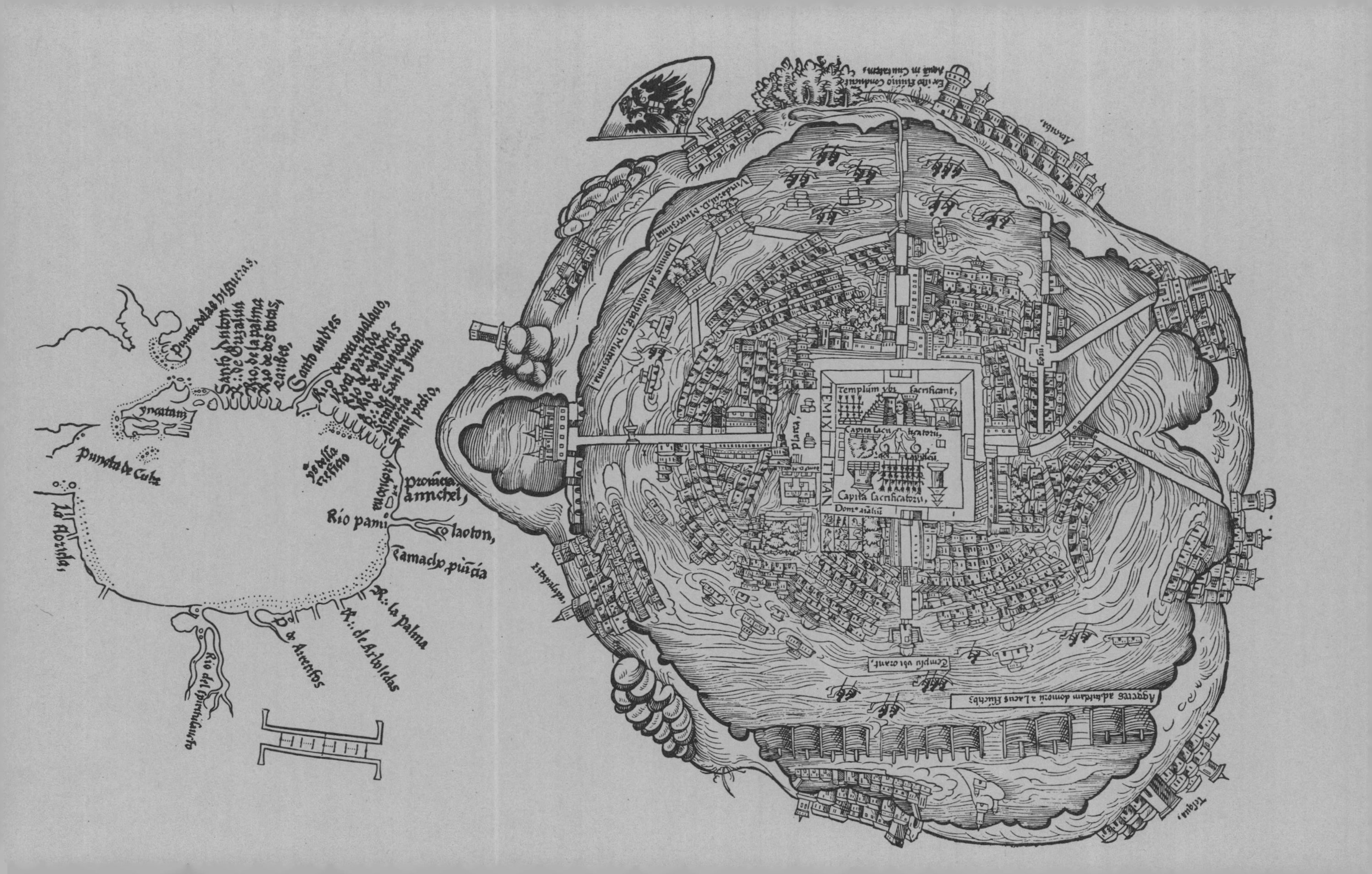

Templum vbi sacrificant,
TEMIXTITAN
Capita sacrificatoru,
Dom^9 aialiu
Platea,
Domus ad voluptate D. Muteczuma
Templu vbi orant,
Aggeres ad ditidam domoru a Lacus fluctibz
Ex isto flumio conducit Aqua in Ciuitatem,
Amaita,
Tacuba,
Punta delas higueras,
Santo Anton
R. de Grijalua
Rio de la palma
Rio de dos totas,
caribes,
Santo andres
Rio de tonoqualano
Rio de alvarado
Rio de vanderas
R. de Sant Juan
Almeria
Sant pedro,
Yucatam
Puncta de Cuba
La Florida,
Rio pami
Prouincia amichel,
Tamacho piuica
R. la palma
R. de Arboledas
Rio del Spiritusancto

The exotic Aztec battle dress included padded cotton armor that had been stiffened by being soaked in brine. The elite warriors—those who took the most captives—wore outfits of eagle feathers or of jaguar skins. Leaders, like the three above, could be easily recognized by elaborate wood and feather frameworks strapped to their backs. Their chief weapons were a decorated round hide shield and the deadly macuahuitl, *a yard-long club studded with obsidian blades.*

idols throughout the various districts of this great city, all fine buildings, in the chief of which their priests live continuously, so that in addition to the actual temples containing idols there are sumptuous lodgings. These pagan priests are all dressed in black and go habitually with their hair uncut; they do not even comb it from the day they enter the order to that on which they leave. . . . Among these temples there is one chief one in particular whose size and magnificence no human tongue could describe. For it is so big that within the lofty wall which entirely circles it one could set a town of fifteen thousand inhabitants. . . .

The images of the idols in which these people believed are many times greater than the body of a large man. They are made from pulp of all the cereals and greenstuffs which they eat, mixed and pounded together. This mass they moisten with blood from the hearts of human beings which they tear from their breasts while still alive, and thus make sufficient quantity of the pulp to mold into their huge statues: and after the idols have been set up still they offer them more living hearts which they sacrifice in like manner and anoint their faces with the blood. Each department of human affairs has its particular idol after the manner of the ancients who thus honored their gods: so that there is one idol from whom they beg success in war, another for crops, and so on for all their needs. . . .

Finally, to avoid prolixity in telling all the wonders of this city, I will simply say that the manner of living among the people is very similar to that in Spain, and considering that this is a barbarous nation shut off from a knowledge of the true God or communication with enlightened nations, one may well marvel at the orderliness and good government which is everywhere maintained.

COPAN: LOST CITY OF THE MAYAS

In 1839 John Lloyd Stephens, a young New Jersey lawyer who had traveled widely in the Middle East and Europe and written two successful books about his experiences, set off on an expedition to Central America. He was accompanied by Frederick Catherwood, an English artist whom he had met three years earlier in London. The two friends hoped to uncover vestiges of an ancient civilization in the uncharted jungles of Honduras and Yucatán. They were spurred on by accounts that had survived from the Spanish colonial period and by notebooks published by Europeans who had gone exploring in the early nineteenth century. One brief narrative, published in 1835, told of a city almost buried in the jungle at Copán, a site in Honduras. Stephens and Catherwood made it their first destination, traveling by steamer, mule, and canoe. They found the spot and promptly bought the ruins from a local landowner for the sum of fifty dollars. There followed weeks spent hacking their way through a tangle of roots and creepers, unearthing terraces, pyramids, courts, shrines, and stelae sculptured with figures and hieroglyphs. And while Stephens explored, Catherwood drew.

From Copán they went on to Chiapas, to the northwest in Mexico, and from there to Yucatán. In 1841 Stephens published a two-volume narrative of their travels, superbly illustrated by Catherwood. Despite its great length, the work became a best seller on both sides of the Atlantic and awakened an interest in the Maya civilization that has never since faltered. Stephens' description of their arrival at Copán makes it easy to understand the book's immediate popularity.

Officially Moctezuma's "guests" in Tenochtitlán, the Spaniards soon forced the emperor to leave his own palace and move into the quarters he had given them, as their prisoner in all but name. Fearing his escape, Cortés even ordered Moctezuma (at right, above) put in chains. The shackles were soon removed, but the Aztec leader later died while under Spanish "protection."

Following a path which our guide cleared for us with his machete, we passed a large fragment of stone elaborately sculptured and half buried in the earth, and came to the angle of a structure with steps on the sides, which insofar as the trees allowed us to make them out, resembled the sides of a pyramid in form and appearance. Diverging from the base of the structure, and working our way through the thick woods, we came upon a square stone column, about fourteen feet high and three feet on each side, sculptured on all four of the sides, from the base to the top, in very bold relief. On the front side was carved the figure of a man (evidently a portrait) curiously and richly dressed, whose face was solemn, stern, and well fitted to excite terror. The design on the opposite side was unlike anything we had ever seen before; the remaining two sides were covered with hieroglyphics. About three feet in front of the column was a large block of stone, also sculptured with figures and emblematical devices. From our guide we learned that the square column was an "idol" [stela] and the block of stone an "altar." The sight of this unexpected monument put at rest once and forever all uncertainty in our minds as to the character of American antiquities, and gave us the assurance that the objects we were in search of were not only interesting as the remains of an unknown people, but were works of art as well, proving, like newly discovered historical records, that the people who once occupied the American continents were not savages. With an interest perhaps stronger than we had ever felt in wandering among the ruins of Egypt, we followed our guide, who, sometimes miss-

The stelae at Copán were called "idols" by the natives who guided Stephens and Catherwood over the site. In two views of "stone idol L" by Catherwood, the monumental face at center displayed to the world for the first time the high-bridged nose and receding chin we now recognize as distinctively Maya.

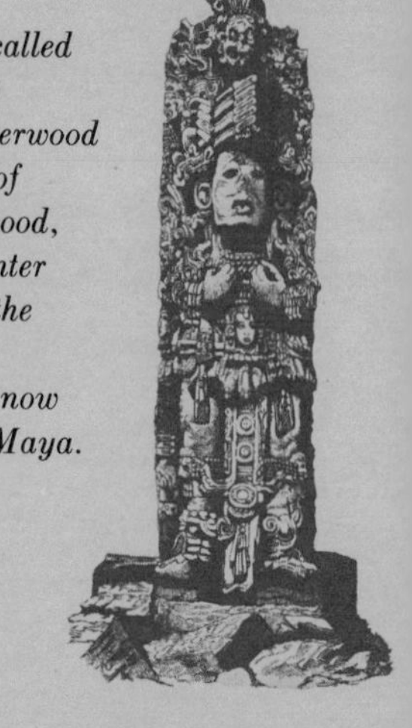

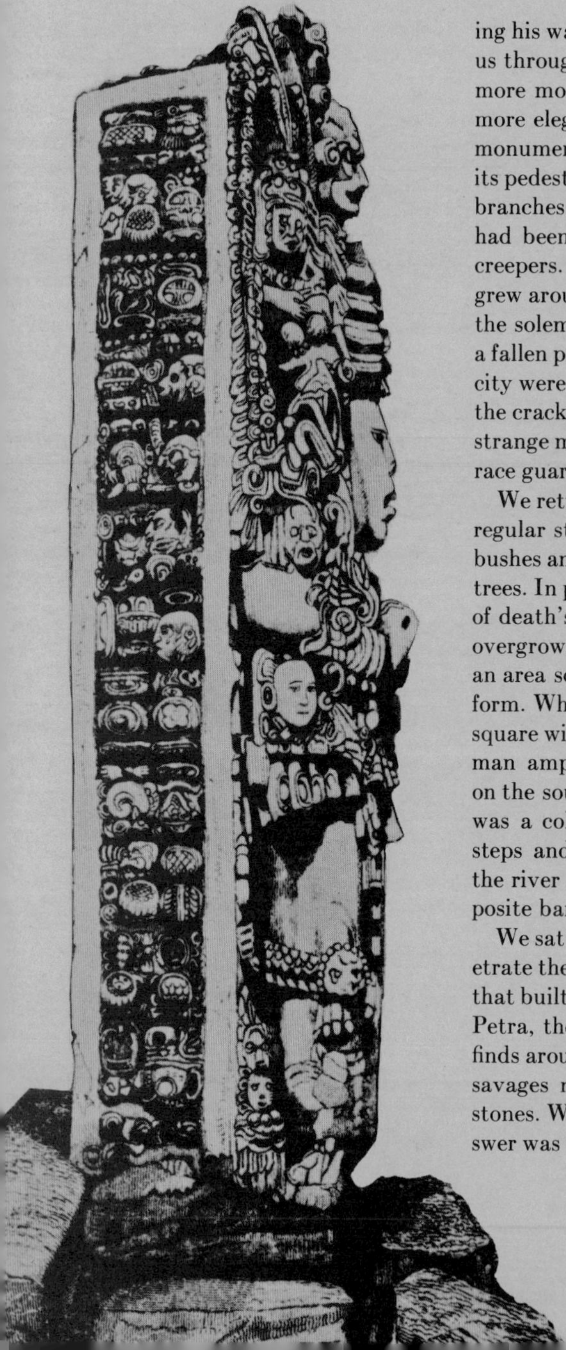

ing his way, with a constant and vigorous use of his machete conducted us through the thick forest, among half-buried fragments, to fourteen more monuments of the same character and appearance, some with more elegant designs, and some in workmanship equal to the finest monuments of the Egyptians. One, we found, had been displaced from its pedestal by enormous roots; another, locked in the close embrace of branches of trees, was almost lifted out of the earth; and still another had been hurled to the ground and bound down by huge vines and creepers. One with its altar before it stood in a grove of trees which grew around it, seemingly to shade and shroud it as a sacred thing; in the solemn stillness of the woods, it seemed a divinity mourning over a fallen people. The only sounds that disturbed the quiet of this buried city were the noise of monkeys moving among the tops of the trees and the cracking of dry branches broken by their weight. . . . Amid these strange monuments, they seemed like wandering spirits of the departed race guarding the ruins of their former habitations.

We returned to the base of the pyramidal structure and ascended by regular stone steps, which in some places had been forced apart by bushes and saplings and in others thrown down by the growth of large trees. In parts they were ornamented with sculptured figures and rows of death's heads. Climbing over the ruined top, we reached a terrace overgrown with trees and, crossing it, descended by stone steps into an area so covered with trees that at first we could not make out its form. When the machete had cleared the way, we saw that it was a square with steps on all the sides almost as perfect as those of the Roman amphitheater. The steps were ornamented with sculpture, and on the south side, about halfway up, forced out of its place by roots, was a colossal head, again evidently a portrait. We ascended these steps and reached a broad terrace a hundred feet high overlooking the river and supported by the wall which we had seen from the opposite bank. . . .

We sat down on the very edge of the wall and strove in vain to penetrate the mystery by which we were surrounded. Who were the people that built this city? In the ruined cities of Egypt, even in the long-lost Petra, the stranger knows the story of the people whose vestiges he finds around him. America, say historians, was peopled by savages; but savages never reared these structures, savages never carved these stones. When we asked the Indians who had made them, their dull answer was "*Quién sabe?*" (Who knows?) There were no associations con-

nected with this place, none of those stirring recollections which hallow Rome, Athens, and "the world's great mistress on the Egyptian plain." But architecture, sculpture, and painting, all the arts which embellish life, had flourished in this overgrown forest; orators, warriors, and statesmen, beauty, ambition, and glory had lived and passed away, and none knew that such things had been, or could tell of their past existence. Books, the records of knowledge, are silent on this theme.

The city was desolate. No remnant of this race hangs around the ruins, with traditions handed down from father to son and from generation to generation. It lay before us like a shattered bark in the midst of the ocean, her masts gone, her name effaced, her crew perished, and none to tell whence she came, to whom she belonged, how long on her voyage, or what caused her destruction—her lost people to be traced only by some fancied resemblance in the construction of the vessel, and, perhaps, never to be known at all. The place where we were sitting, was it a citadel from which an unknown people had sounded the trumpet of war? or a temple for the worship of the God of peace? or did the inhabitants worship idols made with their own hands and offer sacrifices on the stones before them? All was mystery, dark, impenetrable mystery, and every circumstance increased it. In Egypt the colossal skeletons of gigantic temples stand in unwatered sands in all the nakedness of desolation; but here an immense forest shrouds the ruins, hiding them from sight, heightening the impression and moral effect, and giving an intensity and almost wildness to the interest.

Frederick Catherwood, like his friend John Stephens, had been an inveterate traveler but was a stranger to the totally different artistic style of the Maya ruins in the jungles of Central America. Catherwood's ability as a draftsman is evident in these engravings of the stelae at Copán, made from his meticulous on-the-spot drawings. The atmosphere of grandeur and mystery is evoked exquisitely and authentically by these renderings.

TREASURE ENTOMBED AT MONTE ALBAN

On January 9, 1932, Alfonso Caso, head of the Department of Archaeology at the National Museum of Mexico, aimed a flashlight through a hole in the floor of Tomb 7 at Monte Albán, a vast complex of partly buried squares, staircases, pyramids, temples, and tombs in the Oaxaca Valley of southern Mexico. Caso had gone there primarily to help clear the site, and only secondarily to search the tombs. Looters had been busy in them since the eighteenth century and Caso did not expect to discover anything out of the ordinary. To his amazement, the narrow beam of his flashlight illuminated one of the richest archaeological finds ever made in America: the tomb was not only untouched, but it contained an antechamber filled with jeweled treasures of great artistic value.

Before the opening of Tomb 7 next to nothing had been uncovered to

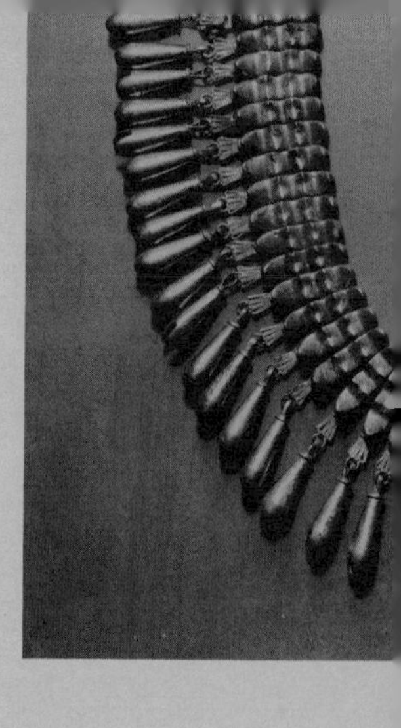

verify the descriptions by early chroniclers of the skill of Mexican goldsmiths and jewelers. The treasures the Spaniards had sent to Europe had been melted down. "Not until today," declared the exultant Caso, "have we been able to form an idea of the great opulence that dazzled the conquerors, and we can affirm that their accounts, which at times seemed exaggerated, conform to, if they are not inferior to, reality."

Analysis of the tomb and its contents revealed an interesting chronology. The burial area had twice been made use of, first by the Zapotec, who constructed it, and then by the Mixtec, who removed the Zapotec bodies and buried their own lords in the tomb. Caso's later researches proved that the Mixtec had seized control of Monte Albán in the early fifteenth century; thus the treasures there had been created by the same people who later, under Aztec rule, had made the ornaments that so dazzled European eyes.

From the earlier, Zapotec occupation of the site at Monte Albán comes this statue of a deity, wearing a monumental headdress and massive earplugs, both typical of the Zapotec style. Monte Albán served as a ceremonial center from about 500 B.C. to A.D. 900 and has retained a certain influence over the surrounding population until quite recently. During his studies, Alfonso Caso found an offering of pottery that was no more than 50 years old.

The Indians of Oaxaca believe that whoever explores a tomb is punished by the spirits of the dead and may become bewitched.

For that reason, when I uncovered Tomb 7 and no traces of sorcery made their appearance, there sprang up in Oaxaca several tales, one of which I mention because of its excellent folklore characteristics.

It is related that one night, when I was in the central plaza of Monte Albán, a well of crystal water opened up at the foot of one of the monuments, and in the middle of it floated a red vessel made from a gourd shell, inside of which was a gilded fish. Instead of being frightened by this marvel, I caught the jug and the fish within it; whereupon the fish informed me of the location of the treasure in Tomb 7. Therefore it was not strange that one to whom the fishes of Monte Albán had spoken should be in no danger of having a spell cast upon him when uncovering the tombs!

We began the exploration of the small mound occupied by Tomb 7 on January 6 of this year [1932] and discovered in its upper part the foundations of some small rooms the floors of which were formed by a heavy layer of mortar. . . .

We made an opening near [the] first finds, and soon the sound of our picks warned us that there was a cavity below and that we were directly over the roof of a tomb; but, before coming to the stones of the burial vault, we still had to break through a second layer of stucco.

About four o'clock in the afternoon of January 9 we began to remove one of the stones which formed the arch of the second chamber of the tomb. Through the narrow aperture, lighted by a flashlight, I could see

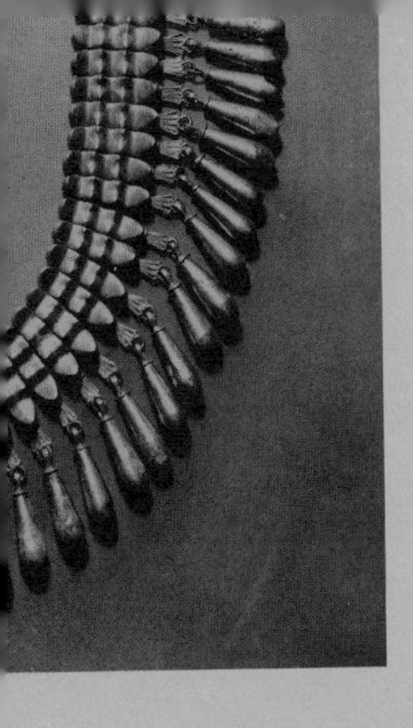

This exquisitely wrought necklace is but one of the 121 gold objects found by Alfonso Caso inside Tomb 7 at Monte Albán. Previously, archaeologists had discovered only a few such treasures from pre-conquest Mexico. Caso's rare find included gold rings, necklaces, and brooches, as well as 24 silver objects. The pieces ranged from extremely simple to highly decorative works, each one a masterly example of the jeweler's art.

a human skull and next to it two vases, one of which seemed to be of black clay with an extraordinary polish. It proved to be a goblet of rock crystal, which appeared black because of the earth within it.

I then removed another stone forming an angle with the first, and the opening was large enough for one of my assistants, Mr. Valenzuela, to squeeze into the tomb. Lighting his way with a flashlight, he descended, and could not restrain his exclamations of astonishment at the riches revealed. My eagerness to behold the wonders of our discovery spurred me to extraordinary effort, and I finally succeeded in overcoming the difficulties of the narrow opening. . . .

On the threshold, or vestibule, separating the two chambers of the tomb, and in the center of a great pile of bones, glittered objects of gold—beads, little bells, etc. Strung on the arm bones of one of the skeletons were ten bracelets, six of gold and four of silver. I found here also what at first appeared to be a tiny vessel of hammered gold ornamented with the figure of a spider, but which subsequently I have come to think was used as a clasp for a belt.

Finally, near the door of the tomb, I saw a golden diadem and next to it the plume, twisted and bent, which at one time served to decorate it. . . .

Valenzuela and I had made this first inspection of the tomb by stepping along some stones projecting irregularly from the ground and permitting us to make the examination without disturbing the objects and human bones. Upon lighting the floor of the tomb, we found it aglow with pearls, golden beads, and innumerable small, flat pieces of turquoise that at one time had composed a rich mosaic. . . . It was impossible to reconstruct it, notwithstanding the fact that my first care was to see if I could save it, even if only in part. . . .

As we left the tomb I realized the incalculable richness of my discovery from a material, an artistic, and a scientific viewpoint. I had no knowledge of any previous discovery in America of such a treasure.

STELA C: THE NEW WORLD'S OLDEST RECORDED DATE

Matthew W. Stirling could well be called the father of Olmec archaeology. While still an undergraduate at the University of California, he began to suspect that an entirely fresh civilization was still to be discovered in Mexico. Twenty-one years later, in 1939, Stirling found proof for his theory, when he led an archaeological expedition to Tres Zapotes in the Mexican state of Veracruz. Months of digging uncovered much material

carved in characteristically "Olmec" style, but the most significant discovery of all was the unearthing of Stela C, the oldest dated monument in the New World.

At first Stirling thought this indicated that the Maya civilization had actually existed far west of the area previously ascribed to them, and that the stela, dated 31 B.C., *was actually an extension back in time of the Maya record. But as he discovered more and more distinctly Olmec objects at Tres Zapotes, and from the even richer site of La Venta, farther east, Stirling became convinced that this was an entirely separate civilization hundreds of years older than the Classic Maya; and that the presence of a Maya Long Count date on Stela C implied that the Olmec, not the Maya, were the originators of this system.*

His discoveries set the archaeological world into a ferment of debate and inaugurated a study of the enigma of the Olmec that continues to this day. Following are portions from a National Geographic *article in which Stirling described his discovery of the all-important Stela C.*

Try as I might, I could distinguish no pattern in the weather-beaten carving on the face of the stela. Thinking I might as well complete the job I had started, I instructed a couple of the men to finish exposing the back of the stela where we had stopped work when the altar was found.

As the men had been cautioned against scarring the monument with the tools, they were on their knees in the excavation, cleaning the mud from the stone with their hands, when one of them spoke up in Spanish:

"Chief! Here are numbers!"

And numbers they were indeed: I don't know how my illiterate workman guessed it, but there, running transversely across the back of our stone, was a beautifully carved row of bars and dots in the form of a Maya calendrical date. Here in front of my eyes was the thing we had all secretly hoped might show up in the course of our work, but which not one of us had had the temerity to expect.

It was obvious that the stone in front of me was a fragment broken from the middle of a large stela on which the date had been originally carved. This fragment had been broken off and reused by the people who had placed it in position as we found it.

It was also apparent that the original stela had fallen on its back and lain in that position for a very long time before being broken up by a later group, for, although the stone is extremely hard, the face

When Stirling's Tres Zapotes expedition uncovered Stela C, the all-important date was in clear relief because the basalt slab had been buried with this side downward. The sculpture on the other side, despite the weathering of centuries, could still be recognized as an Olmec werejaguar mask, reconstructed at left in a drawing by the late Miguel Covarrubias. The stela's value lay in its unique combination of this peculiarly Olmec subject with the early date.

had become much weathered, while the back containing the date was scarcely weathered at all.

Through a remarkable piece of good fortune, when the piece was broken off almost all of the date was on this particular section.

Under the broiling sun I copied the characters and hurried back to camp, where we settled down to decipher them. Before long our calculations were complete. Our date was 6 Eznab 1 Uo of the Maya calendar. Using the day by day correlation of Dr. Herbert J. Spinden, this is equivalent to November 4, 291 B.C., which represents the oldest recorded date ever found in the New World. . . . [The date has subsequently been accepted as 31 B.C., following J. Eric Thompson's correlation, which places dates in the calendar 260 years later than did Spinden.]

It was not difficult to visualize the ancient sculptor at work upon this monument, recording, no doubt, some occasion of great importance to his tribe. One imagines that the design on the face of the stone was first completed, representing the god to which the monument was dedicated.

Then, while gaily bedecked priests and astronomers looked on, the sculptor outlined the glyphs and numerals on the back by abrading grooves around them with his stone tool.

When the proper depth had been reached, the remainder of the surface of the hard stone was painstakingly ground down by the same method until only the glyphs and the bars and dots stood out in sharp, low relief.

The stela was erected and probably stood for a long time, an object of admiration and veneration and a center of religious ceremonies.

Eventually misfortune overtook the tribe or they migrated to other lands. The stela fell on its back, where it lay until, centuries later, another group of people came to occupy the site.

Finding this massive relic and with little respect for the gods of their predecessors, they broke the great stone into several pieces of a size that they could more easily handle. The middle fragment bearing the date, being wider than it was long, they set up on one edge in front of a great stone altar, where once more, serving different gods, the stela looked out on strange ceremonies.

Time passed, the city was again abandoned, and gradually Nature buried the monument with its altar so that it all but disappeared from sight, until just now our spades have brought it to light.

THE ORIGIN OF CORN

All early American civilizations were based on the cultivation of corn. But finding the point in time at which early man first realized that he could domesticate a wild grass into a cultivatable crop puzzled archaeologists until the 1960's, when Dr. Richard S. MacNeish, after years of work, found the oldest corncobs so far known to man. His discovery resulted from a careful narrowing down of the possible areas in central Mexico that would have a sufficiently dry climate, caves deep enough to provide adequate shelter for people to have lived there some 5,000 years ago, and in which the refuse had been undisturbed by the passing centuries. He chose to look in the Tehuacán Valley, and after patient investigation of several dozen unfruitful caves and shelters, he was finally rewarded with one of the most important archaeological triumphs of recent times.

After a long, hot walk along the edge of the mountains, through thick stands of cactus and mesquite, we arrived at the rock shelter. Even from a distance it looked promising. The artifacts and refuse on the surface, the size of the shelter, and the quantity of vegetal material that lay beneath the goat dung covering the floor showed that this was a site to be tested.

From January 21 to January 27 the three of us, Pablo, Hector, and I, tested this cave. Behind a large rock roughly in the center of the shelter we dug a two-meter square to a depth of about two meters, using trowels. We took out everything, including the loose dirt, by bucket loads and put it through a mesh screen to be sure that we missed nothing. Slowly we peeled off the successive strata. The uppermost layer yielded Post-Classic remains; the stratum underlying it contained Classic and a few Formative sherds; then there was a sterile layer. Underneath that was a thick layer which was obviously preceramic. On January 27 after lunch, Pablo, working well down in the preceramic stratum, recovered a tiny corncob no more than an inch long. Only half-believing, I took his place in the bottom of the pit. After a short period of troweling and cleaning away dirt with a paintbrush, I uncovered two more tiny cobs. We held in our hands possible ancestors to modern domesticated corn.

This impression was confirmed a month or two later by Mangelsdorf when he examined the cobs at Harvard University. Still later the cobs were dated to 3610 B.C. ± 250 years. . . . These were the oldest corncobs that had ever been found!

A SENSE OF STYLE

Miguel Covarrubias made a unique contribution to Olmec archaeology. Born in Mexico in 1904, he first won fame as a caricaturist, whose work appeared frequently in American magazines. With success came the opportunity to develop his already overwhelming interest in primitive art and archaeology, and he published several books on these subjects, among them two full-length studies of the native art of North and Central America. He died in 1957, before completing a third study, on South America.

Covarrubias' insistence that Olmec culture must have predated the Maya was a judgment, since confirmed by science, based on his remarkable knowledge and understanding of Olmec art forms. The special portfolio that follows includes drawings taken directly from notebooks in which he sketched Olmec material wherever he could find it. The head above, engraved with werejaguar faces, is carved on a U-shaped stone that could be a replica of the protective pads worn on hands or knees during the sacred ball game. Covarrubias, a champion of the theory of trans-Pacific contacts, was no doubt pleased by its Oriental quality.

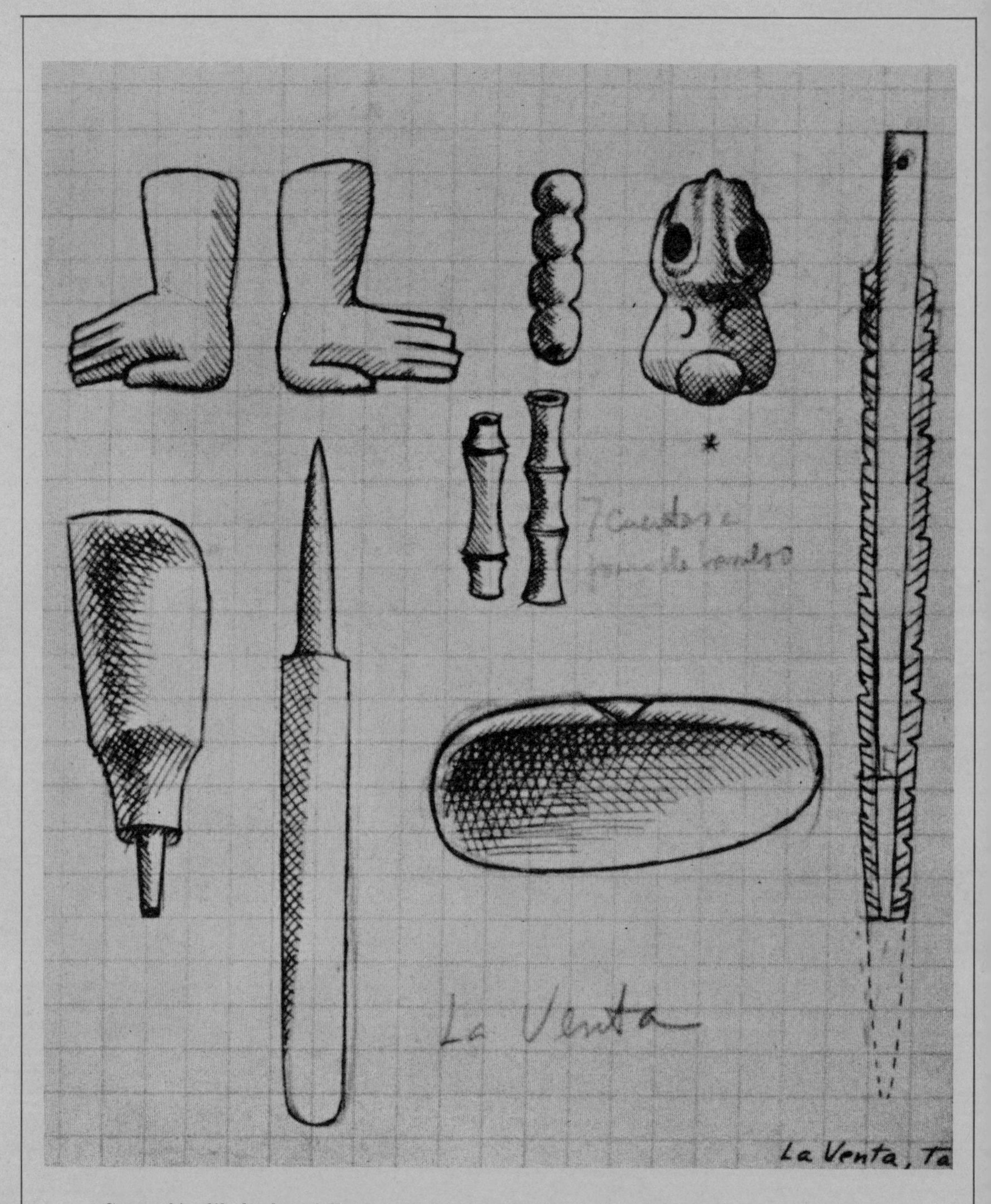

Covarrubias liked to keep fully abreast of the latest archaeological developments, especially excavations on Olmec sites. He visited La Venta during the Stirling expeditions and sketched a group of jade offerings from tombs that were unearthed during the 1942 season. At upper left is a pair of jade hands; beside them is a group of worked jade beads; at far right is a carved replica of a sting-ray spine that was used by the Olmec for ceremonial bloodletting, as were the two sharp-pointed awls at lower left. The oval object between them is a jade clamshell. Following the usual Olmec custom, these objects, made from precious stone hauled from afar, were carefully and minutely worked, and then were deliberately buried.

The strange melancholy that typifies the Olmec style of sculpture is apparent in each of these heads, although stylistically they vary from the primitive incised celt found at La Venta (the oblong shape at left), through the more realistic treatment of an old man's lined face and bald head, which Covarrubias sketched from a private collection, to the two views, side and frontal, of a late Olmec greenstone mask found in Veracruz. This last piece resembles urns made during the early Zapotec period at Oaxaca, which were also strongly influenced by the Olmec style. The mask, one of the most powerful works of art that has yet been discovered in Mesoamerica, is in the Peabody Museum at Harvard University. Covarrubias traveled constantly all over the United States and used every opportunity to sketch Olmec art objects exhibited in collections.

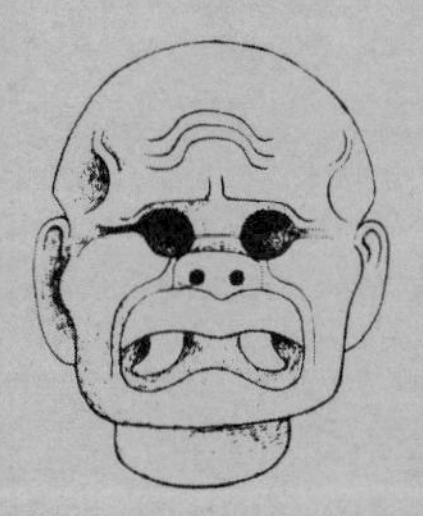

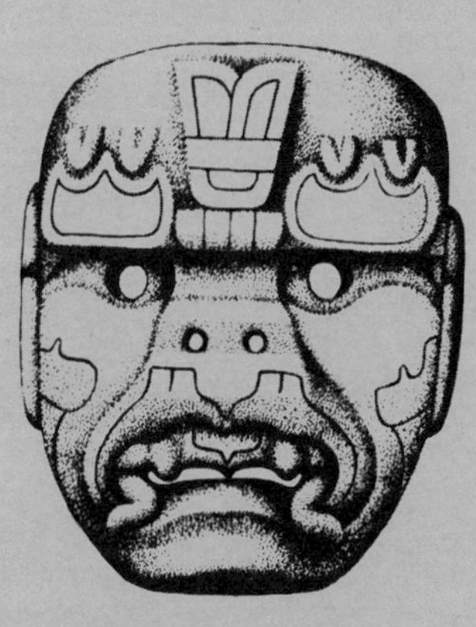

The drawing above, of the 11-inch-long Kunz ceremonial ax in the American Museum of Natural History, possibly represents the Olmec Rain God. It was one of the objects presented by Covarrubias as part of his paper on the Olmec art style, given at the famous round-table conference held in Mexico in 1941, which concluded that the Olmec culture was the first true civilization to appear in Mesoamerica. Covarrubias' paper, the first full treatment of the Olmec style, was worked up directly from the sketches that crammed his notebooks. The figure at left, the so-called Ambassador relief, from La Venta, shows a bearded Olmec carrying what may be a flag and bears four simple hieroglyphs, perhaps the earliest example of writing in the Western Hemisphere. Beneath the relief are two more finds from tombs at La Venta—jade ear ornaments engraved, respectively, with an eagle and a werejaguar motif, seen in profile. Covarrubias made numerous studies of variations on this typically Olmec design, taken from monuments, pottery, and incised celts, some of which are shown on the top half of the opposite page. The striped heads on the upper left and right, however, are not the Rain God, but are identified in this book for the first time as heads of Xipe Totec, the God of Springtime. In later times, Xipe Totec's priests would celebrate the god's rebirth each spring by ceremonially flaying victims and then dancing, dressed in their skins. On the bottom half of the page are abstract motifs of the Fire Serpent, another ancient god, cut into Olmec pottery from Tlatilco. Covarrubias, a pioneer in the study of Olmec iconography, was able to show how many characteristic features of the Rain God honored by later Mesoamerican cultures had developed from an Olmec original.

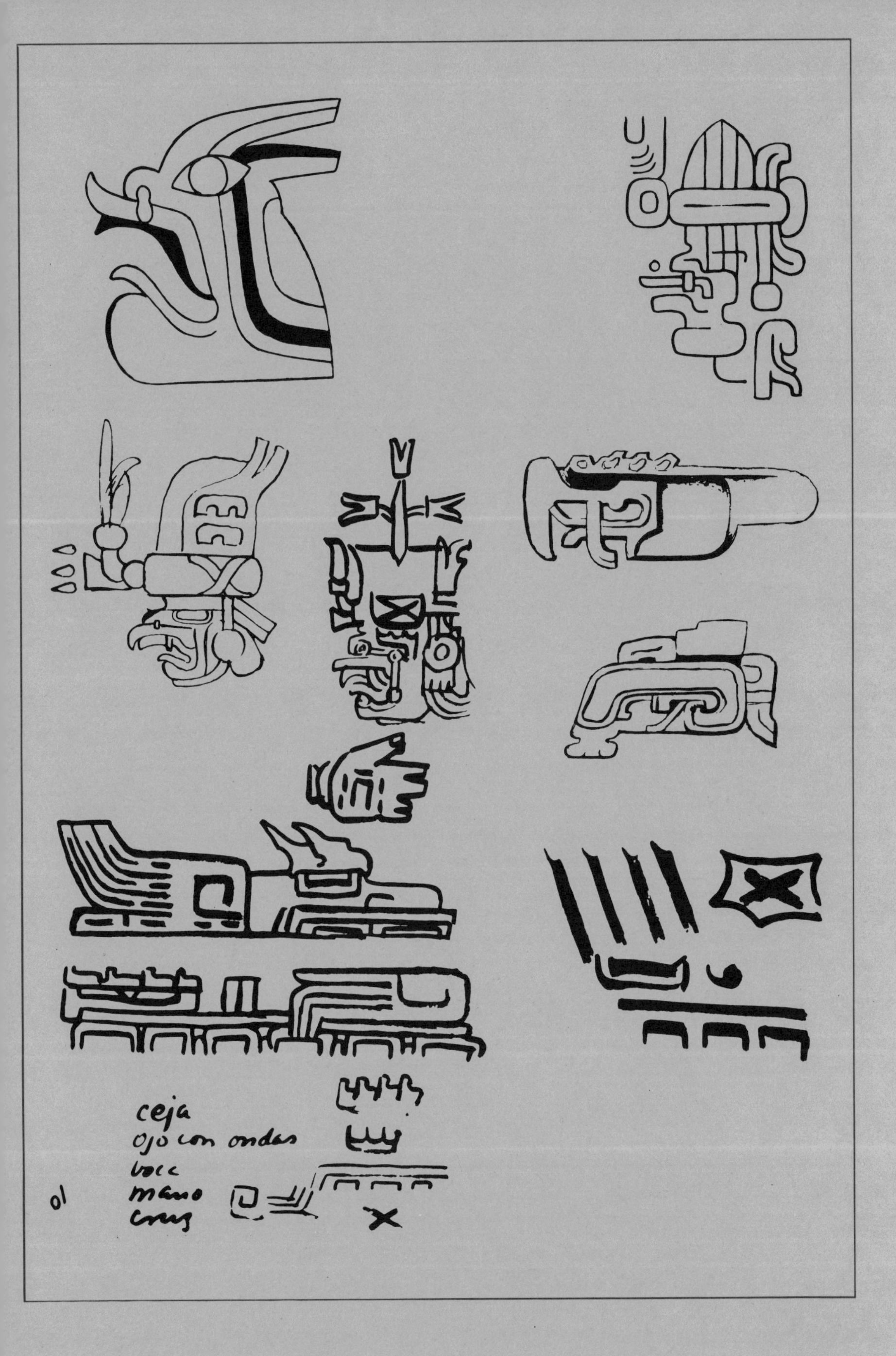
ceja
ojo con ondas
bocc
mano
cruz
01

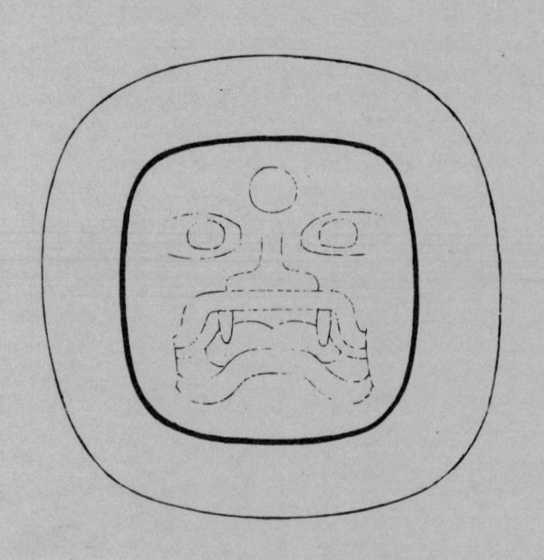

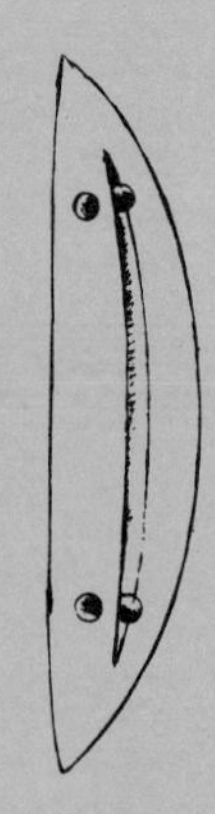

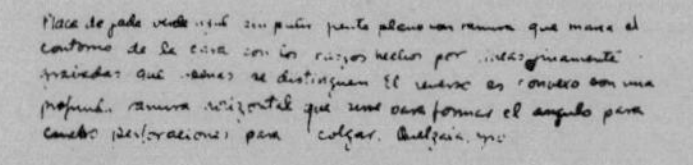

In his notebooks Covarrubias kept drawings of many Olmec pieces in public and private collections (of which his own collection, bequeathed at his death to the Mexican nation, was among the best). In this way he amassed a firsthand knowledge of Olmec art unrivaled by any other authority and informed by his intuitive understanding of the subject. The figure above, of an Olmec god, carved out of blue-green jade, belongs to the Museum of Anthropology in Mexico City. Like many similar pieces in his possession, it comes from Guerrero, which he believed was the birthplace of Olmec culture. At upper left, also from Guerrero, is a jade plaque in the purest Olmec style, with a side view showing the holes pierced in the top that enabled it to be hung around the neck as a pendant. The piece below, a jade effigy of a hand, in New York's Brooklyn Museum, is hollowed out like a box, but the side view shows that it too had drilled holes so that it could be used as a pendant, hanging with the fingers pointing to the left, toward the heart. To the uninitiated, it would be hard to explain exactly why this piece should be Olmec; to an expert with an eye like that of Covarrubias, color, surface treatment, design, workmanship, and over-all "feeling" single it out with unmistakable certainty.

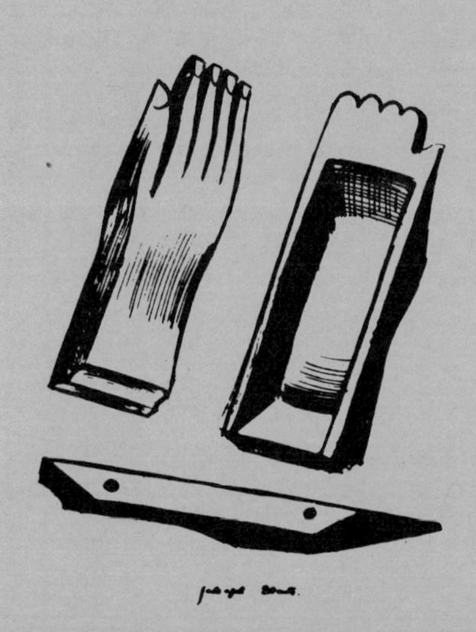

The two apparently pointing figures above are pecked into a boulder at Las Victorias, near Chalchuapa, in El Salvador. This roughly carved monument, over 400 miles southeast of the Olmec heartland of La Venta, represents the ultimate extension of the civilization's power. Covarrubias redrew these figures from a paper on the original find published by the Carnegie Institution of Washington, D.C.

Preoccupied though he was with archaeology, Covarrubias remained a caricaturist at heart. The drawing below, of a contemporary Mixtec Indian from Oaxaca, whose profile struck the artist as characteristically Olmec, catches the essence of a man in very few strokes.
OVERLEAF: *The scene reproduced here for the first time is a gleeful return to satire, this time at the expense of the Classic Maya civilization, whose art forms Covarrubias considered effete. His unwavering belief—in defiance of the generally accepted view that the Olmec culture must derive from that of the more sophisticated Maya—is triumphantly proclaimed by the Olmec-faced "baby" gnawing at the posterior of a "parent" with exaggeratedly Maya features. The accompanying verse leaves no room for misinterpretation. There had been times in the past when Miguel Covarrubias had been almost the sole defender of the theory, which for him was based on incontrovertible artistic evidence, that the Olmec predated the Maya. He had earned the right to put some barbs in his triumphal crown.*

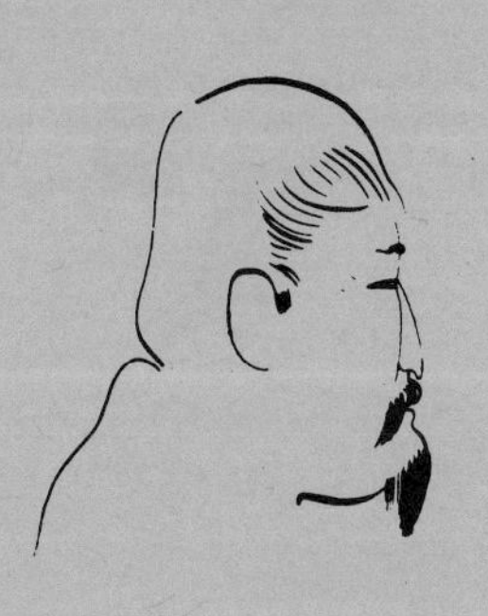

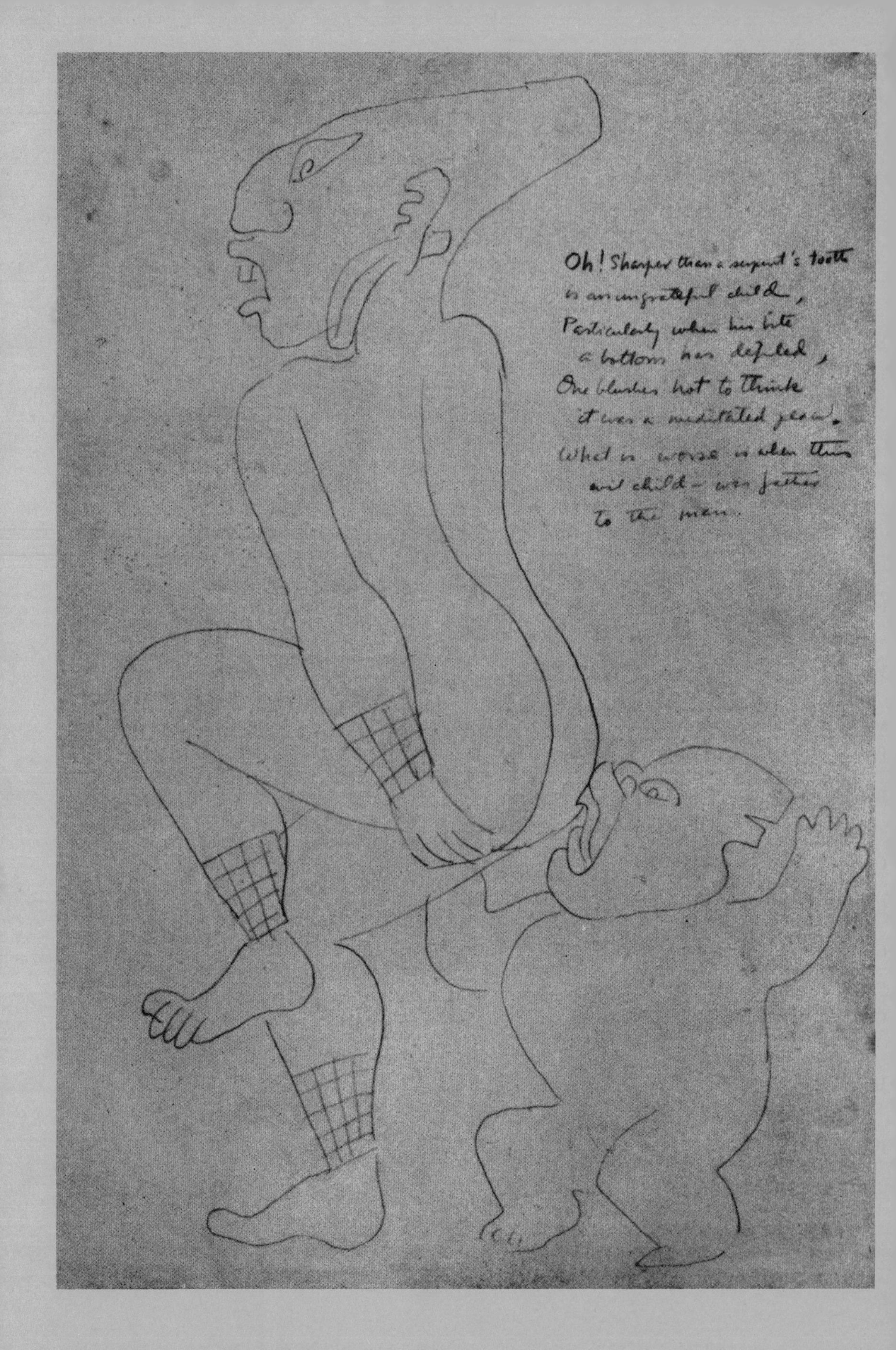
Oh! Sharper than a serpent's tooth
is an ungrateful child,
Particularly when his bite
a bottom has defiled,
One blushes hot to think
it was a meditated plan.
What is worse is when this
evil child – was father
to the man.

FURTHER READING

Asterisk indicates paperback edition.

GENERAL BOOKS ON ARCHAEOLOGY

Brothwell, Don, and Eric Higgs (eds.). *Science in Archaeology.* New York: Basic Books, Inc., 1963.

Chang, Kwang-chih. *Rethinking Archaeology.* New York: Random House, Inc., 1966.*

Heizer, Robert F. *The Archaeologist at Work.* New York: Harper & Row, 1959.

Hole, Frank, and Robert F. Heizer. *Introduction to Prehistoric Archaeology.* Holt, Rinehart and Winston, Inc., 1965.

Wheeler, Robert E. M. *Archaeology from the Earth.* New York: Oxford University Press, 1954.*

MESOAMERICA AND ITS PAST

Benson, Elizabeth P. *The Maya World.* New York: Thomas Y. Crowell Company, 1957.

Byers, Douglas S. (ed.). *The Prehistory of the Tehuacán Valley* (2 vols.). Austin: University of Texas Press, 1967.

Coe, Michael D. *Mexico.* New York: Frederick A. Praeger, Inc., 1962.*

Coe, Michael D. *The Maya.* New York: Frederick A. Praeger, Inc., 1966.*

Covarrubias, Miguel. *Indian Art of Mexico and Central America.* New York: Alfred A. Knopf, Inc., 1957.

Cortés, Hernando. *Five Letters of Cortés to the Emperor.* New York: W. W. Norton & Company, Inc., 1962.*

Díaz del Castillo, Bernal. *The Discovery and Conquest of Mexico.* Translated by A. P. Maudslay. New York: Grove Press, Inc., 1956.*

Paddock, John (ed.). *Ancient Oaxaca.* Stanford, Calif.: Stanford University Press, 1966.

Sahagún, Bernardino de. *Florentine Codex.* Translated by Arthur J. O. Anderson and Charles E. Dibble. Salt Lake City: The University of Utah Press and The School of American Research (Santa Fe, N. Mex.), 1955.

Soustelle, Jacques. *The Daily Life of the Aztecs.* New York: The Macmillan Company, 1962.

Stephens, John L. *Incidents of Travel in Central America, Chiapas, and Yucatán* (3 vols.). New Brunswick, N.J.: Rutgers University Press, 1949.

Wauchope, Robert (ed.). *Handbook of Middle American Indians.* Austin: University of Texas Press, 1964–

Wauchope, Robert (ed.). *They Found the Buried Cities.* Chicago: University of Chicago Press, 1965.

Willey, Gordon. *An Introduction to American Archaeology*; Vol. I, *North and Middle America.* Englewood Cliffs, N.J.: Prentice-Hall, Inc., 1966.

READINGS ON THE OLMEC

Clewlow, C. William, et al. *Colossal Heads of the Olmec Culture.* Berkeley: Contributions of the University of California Research Facility, No. 4, 1967.

Coe, Michael D. *The Jaguar's Children: Pre-Classic Central Mexico.* New York: Museum of Primitive Art, 1965.

Covarrubias, Miguel. *Mexico South: The Isthmus of Tehuantepec.* New York: Alfred A. Knopf, Inc., 1946.

Drucker, Philip. *La Venta, Tabasco: A Study of Olmec Ceramics and Art.* Washington: Bureau of American Ethnology, Bulletin 153, 1952.

Drucker, Philip, et al. *Excavations at La Venta, Tabasco, 1955.* Washington: Bureau of American Ethnology, Bulletin 170, 1959.

Jones, Julie. *Bibliography for Olmec Sculpture.* New York: Museum of Primitive Art, Primitive Art Bibliographies, No. 2, 1963.

Stirling, Matthew W. *Stone Monuments of Southern Mexico.* Washington: Bureau of American Ethnology, Bulletin 138, 1943.

INDEX

Italics indicate illustrations

O

P

Q

R

S